The Old Man

by

Beverly Carradine

First Fruits Press
Wilmore, Kentucky
c2015

The Old Man, by Beverly Carradine

First Fruits Press, ©2015
Previously published by the Kenucky Methodist Publishing Company, 1896.

ISBN: 9780914368045 (print), 9781621714361 (digital), 9781621714378 (kindle)

Digital version at http://place.asburyseminary.edu/firstfruitsheritagematerial/115/

Cover design by Kelli Dierdorf

asburyseminary.edu
800.2ASBURY
204 North Lexington Avenue
Wilmore, Kentucky 40390

First Fruits Press
The Academic Open Press of Asbury Theological Seminary
204 N. Lexington Ave., Wilmore, KY 40390
859-858-2236
first.fruits@asburyseminary.edu
asbury.to/firstfruits

REV. B. CARRADINE, D.D.

THE

OLD MAN.

BY

REV. B. CARRADINE, D.D.,

Author of "A Journey to Palestine," "Sanctification," "The Second Blessing in Symbol," "The Lottery Exposed," "Church Entertainments," "The Bottle," "Secret Societies," and "The Better Way."

L. L. PICKETT,
165 FOURTH AVE.
LOUISVILLE, KY.

Louisville, Ky.:
Kentucky Methodist Publishing Co.
1896.

2

CONTENTS.

CHAPTER I.

THE question engaging many tongues and pens to-day is whether or not there is a principle or nature of sin left in the soul after regeneration.

It is beyond all doubt most important in its bearings upon the religious life. With it stands or falls the doctrine of a second work of grace; for if there be no " remainder of iniquity," then is regeneration all that God does for the soul, and nothing more is to be looked for save a development or growth in grace on our part. If, on the other hand, there is an evil principle left in the heart of the person born of the Spirit, then should all converted people begin at once to groan for deliverance. The fact that such a nature is left in the regenerated heart was never denied, according to Mr. Wesley, until the rise, something over a hundred years ago, of a man named Zinzendorf, who taught that regeneration was purity.

Some one, we believe it was Bramwell, said at the time of the propagation of this strange doctrine that he foresaw that it would be the " devil's big gun," and so it has proved. It is now as a piece of spiritual artillery being shot in many quarters,

(7)

and its echoes fill the land.   Satan certainly made a tremendous leap or change in tactics when, from a teaching of despair that sin could never be taken out of the heart, he swept to the position that in regeneration the soul is made holy.

The explanation of this is evident to the thoughtful.   If the adversary persuades men that regeneration is purity, and that it is also all that God can and will do for the soul, then does he stop them short of the obtainment of the entire sanctification of their moral natures, and so has reached the same end that he did when he taught that sin had to stay in the heart.   In either case sin is covered.   A great change has been made in tactics, but the same end is reached.   Sin is left in the soul.

A great stress is laid by the Zinzendorfian following of the Church to-day on the word " regeneration," and the figure of birth which it stands for.   Regeneration, they say, is the new or spiritual birth.   We are born of God, and such a birth precludes all idea of anything unclean, unholy, or carnal left in the soul.   In this way they endeavor to get rid of the fact of carnality or inbred sin left in the regenerated man.

To establish what they contend for such reasoners are compelled to look to nature for a rule

of analogy, to the Bible for proof of what they say;
and finally to be able to summon human witnesses
in further substantiation and confirmation of the
doctrine. Strange it may appear to some, but not
to all; neither nature nor the Bible nor human testimony will stand by them in the establishment of
their hypothesis.

Let nature be examined first. What can we
find in a physical birth that will bear us out in
claiming, by way of analogy, purity or perfection
for the spiritual birth or regeneration? To our
surprise, on investigation we find that nothing is
born perfect in the physical world. Let a careful examination be made, and the inquirer will
find that no human frame is perfect, that one part
does not exactly correspond to another part, and
that one side of the skull is never the exact coun-
terpart of the other. He will also see that it is the
same way with the face: the two eyes are hardly
ever on a straight line with each other, the ears
frequently differ, one side of the face is not precisely similar to the other, and so on through all
the members of the body. According to this we
have no right to assume perfection in the spiritual
birth from anything we see in the natural world.

In addition to this, we observe that every creature born into the natural world comes into it with the principle of death in its body. Life is there, but so is death. Is it more astonishing to say that goodness is planted in the regenerated man, and this goodness in the face of evil, than to say that a principle of life and one of death and decay is in every creature born into the world?

Going from the idea of perfection in physical birth to that of purity, we find on the very threshold of inquiry that nothing in nature is born clean. The calf after being born is licked clean by the tongue of its mother, while every child that is born has to be washed clean immediately after its birth. According to the testimony of nature, birth is one thing and cleanness is another.

To force the birth figure is to run into folly and absurdity. To say that to be born of God necessitates the experience of holiness, and ground this argument on the figure of natural birth, throws such reasoning open to most absurd conclusions. For instance, to be born of man is to become human; but can we say that to be born of God is to become divine? Are we ever gods? Evidently there is nothing in nature to give us a right to say, by way of analogical reasoning, that spiritual birth means purity or perfection.

Suppose we consider the second argument for purity in regeneration, based on the Bible, and lo! when we turn to the Word of God we discover at the first glance that regenerated people there are urged to go on to perfection. They are told that God wills their sanctification, and can sanctify them wholly and preserve them blameless. Paul told the Christian Hebrews that the object of their discipline as spiritual children was that they might become partakers of "his holiness." All the Epistles are written with a recognition of something to be gotten rid of, and a state or condition to be reached. What the Scripture says positively on the subject will be treated in another chapter of this volume. Enough is seen here to reveal that the Bible gives no authority for claiming purity or holiness at our spiritual birth.

When we look for the third argument, to be materialized in the person of human witnesses who claim purity and perfect love as the direct and immediate result of regeneration, without any subsequent exercise of soul, and following experience, such witnesses cannot be found. Men indeed are found who will write such things on paper in controversy, but it is noticeable that they will not stand up in the great congregation and

claim purity, perfect love, and holiness on the
simple experience of regeneration. It is no trial to
write very loftily with the pen; but, brought face
to face with men and God, the tongue stammers,
the jaws lock, and the witness of the regenerated
man to purity is difficult to be heard in the land.

It strikes the author that one trouble with the
Zinzendorfian wing in the Church is in giving a
meaning to the word " regeneration " that it does
not possess. To get rid of a second work of
grace many in the Church have made the word to
include everything. The word, as found in Eng·
lish and Greek lexicons, means to be born again,
to reproduce, to renovate, etc. In no place or
book do we find the words " freedom," " purity,"
" perfection," or " holiness " given as definitions
of " regeneration." Hence we affirm that a man
has no more right to attach such meanings to the
word than to say that a house means a building,
and also a meadow, field, wood, and plain.

Another mistake with the Zinzendorfians is that,
knowing but one experience in their souls, they
have made all Scripture bend to describe what
they possess. There are passages that describe a
life and experience which they are strangers to;
but, with an assurance that is amazing, they ap-

propriate all; and, when driven to the wall in regard to these passages, say that they describe the
life that they are not living but ought to live, but
that still it is regeneration. A mere boy should
here be able to answer them with the words: "If
this is regeneration described in these lofty passages, and you are regenerated, you should have
them; if you have them not, where are you, and
what are you?" With equal consistency and
truthfulness a man standing on the foothills of the
Alps could say that he was on Mont Blanc, as for
a man to say that he stood on these Alpine peak experiences of the Bible because he was regenerated.

Here I find in the Word of God statements of
"heart circumcision," "dead to sin," "alive unto
God," "the body of sin destroyed," "perfect
peace," "perfect love," "pure in heart," etc.;
and yet here is a man about whose heart the divine circumcising knife has not come; the nails
and thorns and death of the cross are an unknown
spiritual experience; and perfect peace is unknown, and death to the world is unknown; and,
marvelous to say, he claims it all with his pen,
in controversy, while his conscience gives the flat
denial, his best friends are skeptical, and there is
no answering fire from heaven on the part of God.

CHAPTER II.

THERE is a universal consciousness of something of a troublesome and afflicting nature
left in a regenerated heart. This something many
have agreed to call inbred or inbeing sin. Others
call it the "remains of sin." This last expression, if not explained, is apt to be misleading.
The idea naturally conveyed by such a term is
that regeneration destroyed the greater part of the
sinful nature of the individual, but left various
scraps, tendencies, and things of that kind. It
sounds as if an animal had been killed and taken
away, with the exception of his horns, hoofs, and
some pieces of skin and hair. The expression
"remains of sin," unless explained, is apt to con-
vey the idea of a partial regeneration, when Scripture and experience both agree as to a complete
regeneration.

The query arises in the mind: Why should there
be "remains" left in this work? If some engine
or agent of power can destroy the bones, muscles,
and viscera of an ox, why not the horns, hoofs,

(14)

and hair? If regeneration changes me, why should a sinful nature which is called remains of sin be left in us? If we are careful to teach two kinds of sin, the one personal and the other inherited, a wickedness acquired and a depravity received at birth, light will begin to dawn upon the mind. Justification and regeneration deal with personal sin and guilt, and sanctification with inherited depravity.

Of course the objection will be raised as to what regeneration does, if the carnal mind is left. The answer is that regeneration, according to the meaning of the word, is life implanted in a dead soul; and this life may be planted in the face of something else, as a rose can grow in the same clod with a weed. The blunder made by the objector is in making regeneration mean purity, when it really means life.

Another objection urged is that if we are born of the Spirit then we are spiritual, and how can we be carnal? But the Scripture answers this by plainly teaching that in the regenerated life we are both carnal and spiritual. This was said of the Galatian church which had the "flesh" (carnal mind) and the "Spirit" lusting against each other in their hearts. The same thing is stated in re-

gard to the Corinthians whom Paul designates as
"babes in Christ," hence born of God, but adds,
"ye are carnal."

This dark, troubling something within us is not
the remains of our actual sins and personal guilt,
but the inherited bias to sin or evil nature with
which we began life. It is something that cannot
be pardoned, hence is not susceptible of regeneration. It is not subject to the law of God, neither
indeed can be, and so awaits not an impartation of
life, but a movement of destruction and death.
For lack of a better name the Church calls it
inbred sin. In the caption of this chapter we
call it the "Remainder of Iniquity," which is
the true translation of James i. 21, rendered by
King James's translation "superfluity of naughtiness."

Inbred sin is in us all at birth. We are not to
be condemned for this, and are not. It is not our
fault, but our misfortune, that we enter life with
original sin or a bent to evil in us.)

According to Paul, in Romans, justification unto
life is brought to the race through Christ. If we
coming from childhood into years of accountability realize condemnation, it is not for inbred sin,
but for our actual transgressions. Every child,

then, is born in a justified relation to God, but enters the world with inbred sin. If the child dies in
early life. the one work of the Spirit is to sanctify
it, or destroy inbred sin, as the child has done
nothing to need pardon.

If the child lives to years of accountability, according to all human observation and experience,
two things happen: one is that actual or personal
sin is committed, and the other that an acquired
wickedness is added to the inherited depravity.
No one who observes and thinks a moment will
deny this. We by our sinful courses deepen the
malady within, give additional twists to the
crooked nature, and by a series of misdoings add
to the dark stock of trade in the soul. This last
is an acquired wickedness or evil bent. For this
last we are alone accountable.

With this burden of actual transgressions and
acquired evil we come to God with repentance
and faith in Christ, asking for pardon and salvation. In the work of justification and regeneration we obtain the remission of these personal sins
and the washing away of personal guilt, the recti-
fying of the moral wrong we have done to ourselves and the implanting of the divine life in the
soul.

2

Something is left. That something, according to Paul, is "not subject to the law of God, neither indeed can be." He calls it the carnal mind. If this is so, then regeneration did not change it. It is overshadowed, overpowered by a mightier life, but is itself not susceptible of the regenerating grace of God. It awaits another divine work, not of regeneration or life, but of sanctification or death. It is a nature that cannot be pardoned, cannot be justified, and hence cannot be regenerated; for justification must precede regeneration in the kingdom of grace. It is not subject to the law of God—"*neither, indeed, can be.*" It is hopelessly condemned. It is to die, to be crucified, burned out with the baptism of the Holy Ghost, and destroyed. But regeneration is neither crucifixion, the baptism of fire, nor destruction; it is a birth and life.

To make the matter plainer, we use a simple illustration. A boy starts to roll up a big ball of snow, by taking a large rock or chunk of wood to begin with. In a little while it becomes huge with its additions and accumulations. Now put this ball under the sudden dash of a waterfall, and the snow all at once disappears, but the original rock or chunk is left. So we start out with in-

bred sin at birth.   In a few years we add to it by
our own misdeeds.   What a dark life we soon roll
up!   Under the " washing of regeneration " all
these personal sins and acquired evil are swept
away; but inbred sin, the original rock or chunk
is left; and let men say what they will, they all
feel that it is there.

Now, as we said a few paragraphs back, we are
not condemned for inbred sin at our birth.   No
man is sent to hell because of what Adam did to
him and in him, but for what he did himself.   But
while this is so, yet when God reveals to us this
inbred or original sin remaining in us, and shows
the way of deliverance, then from that moment we
become responsible for its existence in our souls.
In a sense our sheltering it in our hearts becomes
a personal sin, and we are in danger of going into
shadow and condemnation.

To illustrate this responsibility we bring forward
a case.   Suppose a keg of powder has been
placed under a man's house and right beneath the
hearth where a fire is burning, but he is ignorant
of its presence there.   After awhile a coal drops
upon the keg, burns its way through the top, and
there is a terrible explosion, in which the man's
family is destroyed.   Fearful as is the occurrence,

no one condemns the man. But suppose he had
been told that the keg of powder was there, and he
saw it for himself in its proximity to the fire, and
went away without removing it.   Then, when the
explosion took place and his family were killed,
everybody would condemn him and say that he
was a guilty man.

He who is born with inbred sin is not regarded
as being guilty for that, because another hand, so
to speak, placed it there.   But when God, by his
Spirit, reveals the evil nature, its danger and the
way of deliverance, and the man fails to seek and
secure the deliverance provided for and offered
him, then does he become a guilty man and is to
be condemned both by men and God.

Here, then, is the "remains of sin."   Not the
remains of personal transgressions, for they are all
pardoned.   Not the remains of personal guilt, for
that is all washed away in regeneration.   Not
fragments of tempers, thoughts, and desires that
the grace and power of God could not altogether manage or dispose of—that would teach a
partial regeneration.   Not the remains of sin at all
in these senses, but the "remainder of iniquity"
that carnal mind, with which we entered the
world, which is unsusceptible of regeneration, and

which, therefore, is left in the regenerated heart, overshadowed, overpowered indeed, by the grace of God, but still there, and awaiting that death and destruction which comes in sanctification.

CHAPTER III.

ONE class of proof of inbred sin is seen in the confession and testimony of Christians. It is to be found in biographies and autobiographies, in letters, and oral acknowledgments. Out of all countries, and from all ages of the world, comes the confession of regenerated people that they recognize in their hearts a dark indwelling something that brings sorrow, humiliation, and often condemnation.

The admission is that it is a rooted something, not a temptation, not a susceptibility to temptation; but a movement, bias, principle, or nature of evil located in the soul; that it is struggled with, wept over, watched against, in vain; that the heart tries to expel it, but, while subdued and kept under, it is still felt to be there, and at the most unexpected occasions asserts itself in thought, desire, word, and action.

Out of a host of witnesses that we could cite, of eminent people, we quote from one well known to many thousands—viz., Bishop McKendree. After writing about his conversion to Bishop Asbury, he adds; " Not long after, I heard Mr. Gibson preach on sanctification. I examined my heart, and found *remaining corruption*."

In a holiness convention in one of the Southern States the author had pointed out to him a superannuated Methodist preacher who had greatly hindered the holiness movement in that place. One morning, at the close of the convention, the gentleman arose under evident conviction and said: " You all know me. You know that I am a child of God, and have been serving him for over forty years. Yet I am compelled in truth and honesty to make this confession, that in all these years I have felt something away down in here that I wished was out." As he stood boring his finger like an auger over his breast, the action was even more impressive than the words he had uttered.

In a certain Western city, during one of the revivals services held by the writer, a Congregational preacher swept into the blessing of sanctification. When he first spoke in the testimony meeting he told the audience that he had all that the evangelists preached and possessed, and was a happy man. He looked so; and with his good, shining face he was more likely to prove a stronger adver-

sary to the doctrine that was being preached than
violent opposition. But the revelation came to
him; and one day while he was singing in the audience he sunk suddenly into his seat, and covered his face with his hands. God had poured
in the light at last, and he saw that dark something
in his soul that Christ wants to take out of every
believer. We copy his own statement, written a
few weeks afterwards, for a holiness paper. He
said: "I attended the meetings from the outset as
much as my pastoral duties would permit, with the
intention of getting what benefit I could from
them. I did not believe the doctrine preached,
but was hungering and thirsting for righteousness. On the evening of the 26th, when the call
was made for those who had been sanctified to
rise, I stood up, feeling that I had consecrated
myself afresh to God, and was set apart anew by
him to his service. This was what I understood
by sanctification. While I was standing singing,
and feeling quite happy, suddenly like a flash
conviction came to me; then followed another
and another revelation of things that I must do,
idols in my heart that must be destroyed, impuri-
ties that must be cleansed. I sank down in my
chair, and felt as if I were sinking through the

floor into the earth   All this took place in two or
three minutes.   Then when the self-revelation
was completed the strangest sensations followed.
It seemed as though something like the fingers of
a very soft hand gently separated something from
me, and it fell off from me into the earth.''   This
remarkable experience from an intellectual and
cultivated minister of the gospel speaks for itself.
He went on to describe the '' filling up '' of his
soul, but we only have need here for the confession of inbred sin.

Ministers of the gospel, who were true and loy-
al men, have made the following acknowledgments in the author's presence: One said that
'' the praise of men was as sweet as dripping
honey '' to him.   A second said: '' I cannot keep
from jerking my horse.''   A third admitted: '' I
cannot keep from speaking irritably and roughly
to my wife.''   A fourth confessed that the great
pang of his heart was the memory of having spoken harshly, and habitually also, to his wife, who
was now in heaven.   A fifth said that he had
again and again slapped his little boy because he
came around him when he was preparing a sermon.   A sixth declared that he would have revenge on a certain bishop for an appointment that

he had received. A seventh never opened his Bible at a great camp meeting during the whole ten days that it lasted. An eighth, at the same camp meeting, he retired to rest night after night without kneeling in prayer. These last four are among the strongest opponents to the present holiness movement that we have; and yet no man, either out of or in the Church, questions the fact that they are regenerated men.

These things are not written in a fault-finding spirit, or as a personal attack upon these brethren, but simply to call attention to the fact that there must be something left in the soul to produce such results as have just been mentioned.

A second human proof is found in the experience of Christians.

In the first gladness of the hour of salvation the young convert dreams not that anything of evil is left in him. He may have gone on for days and weeks in his blissful ignorance; but the discovery comes at last, as it comes to all.

Young Christians realize to their amazement this dark indwelling something. It is a mistake to call it temptation. The wonder and grief arise from the consciousness of an inward proneness to do wrong. Older Christians, after years spent in the service of God, find the same thing in their souls, to their profound pain and humiliation. Many are puzzled over it, and all lament the indwelling nature,

A converted Indian described it in the words, " I find two Indians in me: one good Indian and one bad Indian; " while regenerated people everywhere, if perfectly honest, must confess to the existence of a Sunday man and a Monday man; and the Monday man does not appear at times to be at all closely related to the Sunday man.

For the glory of God the author testifies to his own personal discoveries in this line: My conversion was bright and thorough. No one doubted my spirituality in the ministry. For twelve years or more preceding my sanctification I never put my head on my pillow at night without first obtaining a sense of my acceptance with God. My first vivid impression of sin in my heart was through a sudden loss of temper, months after my conversion. At the time it occurred I was never more faithful in my Christian duties, and was praying four and five times a day on my knees. The thing that startled me was that when the temper burst forth it came out *full-grown*. There was no " blade, ear, and full corn in the ear "

process. It came out the *full ear!* I was much
shocked, and did not know how to account for it.
A year after the same thing occurred. Four
years after that it flamed out again in a protracted
meeting, where I became vexed with the stub-
bornness of the unconverted. On a fly leaf in my
Bible I wrote down a number of dark things that
I found in my heart, and which I felt ought not to
be there. One was levity, another uncharitable
speech, and still another an unsanctified ambition.
I did not regard these to be temptations, but felt
that they were rooted in me somehow. This was
years before I had thought about or formed an
opinion concerning sanctification. My prayer
was continually that God would take these
things out.

As the years rolled by I added to the dark list
on the fly leaf of my Bible until I counted sixteen
specifications in the bill of charges, which, under
the light of the Spirit, I had made out against myself. On going to New Orleans I was made so
to suffer through a wrong done me by an individual that I had to lie for hours on my face in
prayer to keep resentment and hate from having a
permanent lodgment.

From these and other things I saw, as Mr.

Wesley calls it, "the ground of my heart." The view sickened and humbled me. Some months after this, while preaching at the Seashore Camp Ground on the " Disobedient Young Prophet," I became convicted under my own preaching of the need of a deeper cleansing than I had ever before received, and an induement of power along with it. Fired with this feeling, I leaped on the altar, and called for those who felt as I did to meet me there. Some that read these lines will remember the remarkable scene that followed.

Nearly nine months after this, during a meeting held in my own church in New Orleans, I was praying alone in the altar, when my prayer was turned in on myself, and my soul was literally wrenched in an unutterable agony to be rid of a dark indwelling something that made itself felt as I prayed. I shall never forget the twist of soul in this fruitless effort through prayer to expel this something.

Of course I will be accused here of making in-bred sin a tangible and material thing—in fact, an entity; but my reply to such objectors is, Only wait until the light comes in upon you, as it did to the prophet Isaiah, and to many others since that day, and there will be at once a most painful but thorough understanding of an experience that seemed before to be without foundation.

This dark something has been taken out of my heart, and has been gone six years, since the morning of my sanctification. Let men speculate and be as skeptical as they will, but the writer knows that for six years he has had perfect inward deliverance and rest. Free moral agency is left; susceptibility to temptation remains; but that dark, sad something that used to burden the heart and destroy the joy and disturb the mind and fret the spirit—that, thank God, is gone.

CHAPTER IV.

THIS proof of inbred sin is found in the writings of the standard authors, articles of religion, and creeds of every one of the branches of Christ's Church in the world.

Mr. Wesley once remarked that there is not a single denomination or Church on earth but recognizes remaining sin in the regenerated heart, by providing in their teachings for its removal some time in the future. Some place this deliverance from sin in the near, others in the remote future, and still others in eternity itself; but the fact that they all teach that purity is to follow pardon, some time or another, is unquestionable proof of the fact that these same Churches recognize a sinful nature or principle left in the regenerated soul.

THE PROTESTANT EPISCOPAL CHURCH.

The Ninth Article of Religion says: "Original sin standeth not in the following of Adam, but it is the fault and corruption of the nature of every man that naturally is engendered of the offspring

of Adam; and this *infection of nature doth remain*, yea in those that are *regenerated.*"

THE PRESBYTERIAN CHURCH.

The Confession of Faith (Chap. IX., Sec. 4)
has this to say: " When God converts a sinner,
and translates him into a state of grace, he freeth
him from his natural bondage under sin; yet by
reason of his *remaining corruption* he doth not
perfectly, nor only, will that which is good, but
doth also will that which is evil." In Chapter
XIII., Sections 2 and 3, we have this additional
statement made: " There abideth still some rem-
nants of corruption in every part, whence ariseth
a continual and irreconcilable war."

THE CATHOLIC CHURCH.

The teaching of this body is well known, that
by the fires of purgatory the soul is cleansed and
freed from remaining filthiness. This purification
by the fires of another world is a plain statement
of something left in the pardoned soul of a sinful
or evil nature. The Council of Trent, whose
canons are the highest standards of doctrine and
discipline of the Roman Catholic Church, at its fifth
session, held June 17, 1546, issued this confession:
" But this holy synod confesses and is sensible that
in the baptized there remains concupiscence, or an

incentive (to sin), which, whereas it is left for our exercise, cannot injure those who consent not, but resist manfully by the grace of Jesus Christ.''

THE LUTHERAN CHURCH.

We take the following from the Augsberg Confession: '' Since the fall of Adam all men are born with a *depraved nature*, with *sinful propensities*. That the Son of God truly suffered, was crucified, died, and was buried that he might reconcile the Father to us, and be a sacrifice not only for original sin, but also for all the actual sins of men. That he also *sanctifies those who believe in him* by sending into their hearts the Holy Spirit.'' Remaining sin after justification, and its final removal, is here plainly taught.

THE CONGREGATIONAL CHURCH.

The following is taken from their Confession of Faith: '' We believe that those who are thus regenerated and justified grow in sanctified character through fellowship with Christ, the indwelling of the Holy Spirit, and obedience to the truth; that *a holy life is the fruit* and evidence of saving faith.'' In the words which we Italicize we notice that a holy life is said to be the *fruit* of saving faith. In a word, the tree has been planted in

3

regeneration, and afterwards comes holiness, a distinct thing.

THE SHAKERS.

We quote from a volume which, summing up their teachings, says: " Shakers hold that the true Christian Church is a congregation of souls *baptized* with that degree of Christ's Spirit which harvests them from the selfish, sinful elements of the world, absolves them from the bondage of sin and the power of sinful temptations." Let the reader remember that regeneration is a birth, but that the reference here is to a spiritual baptism which delivers from remaining sin.

THE SALVATION ARMY.

We take from their published doctrine: " We believe that it is the privilege of all believers to be wholly sanctified; we believe that after conversion there remains in the heart of the believer *inclination to evil* or *roots of bitterness*, which, unless overpowered by divine grace, produce actual sin; but that these *evil tendencies* can be entirely taken away by the Spirit of God."

THE CUMBERLAND PRESBYTERIAN CHURCH.

We quote from their Confession of Faith (Sec. 57): " Growth in grace is secured by personal consecration to the service of God, regular attention to the means of grace, the reading of the Holy Scriptures, prayer, the ministrations of the sanctuary, and all known Christian duties. By such means the believer's faith is much increased, his *tendency to sin* weakened, *the lusts of the flesh mortified*, and he more and more strengthened in all saving grace and in the practice of holiness, without which no man shall see the Lord."

THE REFORMED CHURCH OF GERMANY.

In the Formula of Concord (Art. IV., Sec. 8) we read, " But we acknowledge that this liberty of spirit in the elect children of God is not perfect, but is as yet weighed down with manifold infirmity, as St. Paul laments concerning himself about this matter (Rom. vii. 14–25; Gal. v. 17); and again (Art. VI., Sec. 8), "And they that believe according to the spirit of their mind have perpetually a struggle with their flesh—that is, with corrupt nature, which adheres in us even till death; and on account of the old Adam which remains fixed in the intellect and will of man and in all his powers, there is need that the law of God should always shine before man, that he may not frame anything in matters of religion under an impulse of self-devised devotion, and may not choose out ways of honoring God not instituted by the Word of God."

THE SWISS CHURCH.

In the Helvetic Confession is the following statement: " Secondly, in the regenerate there remains infirmity; for sin dwells in us, and the flesh struggles against the spirit in renewed persons; even unto the end the regenerate are not able at all readily to accomplish what they undertake. This is confirmed by the apostle in the Epistle to the Romans, chapter vii., and Galatians v."

THE BAPTIST CHURCH.

This religious denomination is remarkably clear in its teaching in this regard. We quote from " Christian Doctrines," a compendium of their theology, by Dr. Pendleton, the most orthodox of Baptists. In chapter xxi., on sanctification, and page 300, we find these words: " Regeneration breaks the power of sin and destroys the love of sin, so that whosoever is born of God doth not commit sin in the sense of being the slave thereof; but it does not free the soul from *the presence and pollution of sin*. Alas! the regenerate know full well that *sin is in their hearts*. This accounts for the Christian warfare. This conflict implies the *remains of sin* in the believer."

The Methodist Church is so full in its statements of inbred sin left in the regenerated man that we devote the next chapter to showing up some of her teachings in this regard.

A longer enumeration of the Churches could be easily secured, but what is said here is enough to awaken concern and inquiry in the most thoughtless, when every religious denomination is seen dividing or separating pardon from purity, and locating or setting the time for the obtainment of the last, somewhere in the future, in growth, at death, or in purgatory.

The founder of the Methodist Church, Mr. Wesley, says that no one ever taught differently until the appearance of Count Zinzendorf.

It does seem very wonderful to the writer that at this late hour of the world's religious history we should find preachers turning from the teaching of all the Churches, and adopting the doctrines of one man, who, in his bold affirmations, sets himself up not only against all Christendom, but, as we shall see, against the Scriptures as well.

Zinzendorf, as the reader knows, claimed that regeneration is purity, thus denying remaining sin in the heart after conversion, and so removing the necessity for a second work of grace.

The author's opinion of Zinzendorf is that he underestimated a justified religious childhood; and when afterwards, upon a complete consecration, he received the blessing of sanctification, he mistook it for regeneration, and so called it, and wrote accordingly. This mistake the writer has known a number of people to make; and the reader can well see how, in the absence of clear teaching on the subject, such mistakes could be made.

Let this be as it may, it certainly should occur to all that the statement of a solitary individual like Zinzendorf, given for the first time in the eighteenth century, should certainly deserve less credence than the deliberate utterance of all the Churches, in all the ages, in all the countries, that sin in some kind of form is left in the regenerated heart.

CHAPTER V.

THE recognition of inbred sin, or the cleansing from the heart of the regenerated man of remaining sin, is seen in the "Wesleyan Catechism," No. 2, where, after asking and answering the question, "What is regeneration?" and defining it as "that great change which God works in the soul when he raises it from the death of sin to the life of righteousness," then comes later on the question, "What is entire sanctification?"

The answer is: "The state of being *entirely cleansed from sin* so as to love God with all our heart and mind and soul and strength, and our neighbor as ourselves." According to this definition perfect cleansing or purity was not obtained in regeneration. But in the blessing of entire sanctification we are *"entirely cleansed"* and as a result have not only purity of heart, but perfect love to God and man. The whole thing we contend for is in the answer quoted from our standard catechism.

The Hymn Book.

Let the reader take up the hymnal of the Methodist Church and turn to the department devoted
to the Christian life and experience and see for
himself the recognition of inbred sin in the confessions, lamentations, battlings with, and calling
on God for deliverance from some kind of indwelling sinful principle or nature.

One hymn well known to all reads as follows:

> Prone to wander, Lord, I feel it,
> Prone to leave the God I love.

Here the affirmation is made that God is loved,
which establishes the fact of the regenerated condition. Then comes the lament over a proneness
to wander away and leave God. This "proneness" is what we are trying to expose. Proneness to leave God is one thing, and the power to
leave God is another. Every free moral agent
has the power to turn from and forsake God. A
Christian may realize this power and not feel the
proneness. A wife has the power to leave her
husband's heart and home, but may not feel the
inclination or proneness to do so. When the
Church sings

> Prone to wander, Lord, I feel it,

it is not singing of free agency, but about a nature, principle, or bias to evil that can as certainly be removed by divine power as was the personal sins and guilt which were washed away by the same omnipotence.

Let the reader go farther in the hymn book and brood on such lines as the following in No. 411:

> Remove this hardness from my heart,
> This unbelief remove.

And what is this but a confession of what every regenerated man has felt in his Christian life; an unbelief that at times astonished him, and a "hardness" that aroused the query, "Can I be a child of God, and have such a stony feeling in my soul?" All of which is answered by Ezekiel when he speaks of the "stony heart" which is not to be pardoned or grown out, but taken out by divine power. "I will take the stony heart out of your flesh."

How the doctrine of remaining sin crops out in such lines as this,

> Strange flames far from my heart remove;

and again in No. 426,

> The word of God is sure
>   And never can remove;
> We shall in heart be pure
>   And perfected in love:
> Rejoice in hope, rejoice with me,
> We shall from all our sins be free.

Then in 441:

> Scatter the last remains of sin
>   And seal me thine abode;
> O make me glorious all within,
>   A temple built for God!

This is certainly a very strange hymn if regeneration brings purity.   In No. 445 we read:

> Break off the yoke of inbred sin,
>   And fully set my spirit free:
> I cannot rest till pure within,
>   Till I am wholly lost in thee.

In full expectation and pantings of spirit for the blessing No. 447 is written:

> O that in me the sacred fire
>   Might now begin to glow,
> Burn up the dross of base desire,
>   And make the mountains flow!
>
> O that it now from heav'n might fall
>   And all my sins consume!
> Come, Holy Ghost, for thee I call;
>   Spirit of burning, come!
>
> Refining fire, go through my heart,
>   Illuminate my soul,
> Scatter thy life through ev'ry part
>   And sanctify the whole.
>
> No longer then my heart shall mourn,
>   While, purified by grace,
> I only for his glory burn,
>   And always see his face.

It would be easy to quote voluminously from Clarke, Fletcher, Watson, and Benson, but we prefer to select from

MR. WESLEY.

Certainly as the founder of the Methodist Church he has a right to be heard, and ought to be able to represent her doctrinal views. We quote from his sermon on "Sin in Believers." The very title is significant. After describing the grace of regeneration in a man, he says: "But was he not freed from all sin, so that there is no sin in his heart? I cannot say this; I cannot believe it; because Paul says to the contrary. . . . And as this position—that there is no sin in a believer, no carnal mind, no bent to backsliding—is thus contrary to the Word of God, so it is to the experience of his children. These feel a heart bent to backsliding, a natural tendency to evil, a proneness to wander from God. They are sensible of sin remaining in the heart, pride, self-will, unbelief; and of sin cleaving to all they speak or do." "Although we are renewed, cleansed, purified, sanctified, the moment we truly believe in Christ, yet we are not then renewed, cleansed, purified, altogether; but the flesh, the evil nature, still remains, though subdued, and wars against the Spirit."

Again in Mr. Wesley's book on "Christian Perfection" (pages 37 and 38), after describing the blessedness of the regenerated life, he adds: "And now first do they see *the ground of their heart;* which God before would not disclose to them, lest the soul should fail before him and the spirit which he had made. Now they see all the hidden abominations there—the depths of pride, self-will, and hell." Still again, on pages 80 and 81, is the answer to the question, " When may a person judge himself to have attained this? "

Ans. " When, after having been fully convinced of *inbred sin* by a far deeper and clearer conviction than that he experienced before justification, and after having experienced a gradual mortification of it, he experiences a total death to sin and an entire renewal in the love and image of God, so as to rejoice evermore, to pray without ceasing, and in everything to give thanks."

But some say that Mr. Wesley changed his views before he died, and that this change took place in the year 1784, and is seen in his abridgment of the Seventh Article of Religion, where the words teaching inbred sin were left out.

This as an argument proves too much, for we find that he left no article on heaven or hell.

Why does not some one say that Mr. Wesley changed his views here, concluding, doubtless, that there were no such places!

In complete refutation of this we call attention to the footnote of the Church Editor on the first page of " Christian Perfection: " " It is not to be understood that Mr. Wesley's sentiments concerning Christian perfection were in any measure changed *after the year* 1777."

Mr. Wesley himself says, on page 39 of " Christian Perfection: " " Whether our present doctrine be right or wrong, it is, however, the same which we taught from the beginning."

But still more overwhelming is the proof that he never changed, by reference to his own writings up to the last year of his life.

Mr. Wesley died in 1791. Certain people say that " he changed his views " in 1784. Let the reader carefully observe the dates and language of the following extracts from his writings, and see the truth for himself, and be at rest on this subject forever.

We all know that the doctrine of a second work of grace depends upon the fact of a sinful principle or nature left in the soul after regeneration. If the heart is made pure at conversion, then there

is nothing but a gradual and everlasting development to take place, and there is no need for any
exhortation to be given Christians but to grow in
grace.

Instead of this, however, we find Mr. Wesley
continually urging believers on to the obtainment
of a blessing which he calls " perfection," " perfect love," and " full sanctification." If he
" changed his views," nothing of this kind ought
to have fallen from his lips or pen after the year
1784, as we see in the following extracts:

1785.

"At our love feast in the evening at Redwell
several of our friends declared how God had
saved them from *inbred sin* with such exactness,
both of sentiment and language, as clearly showed
that they were taught of God." (Journal.)

"And it will be well as soon as any of them find
peace with God to exhort them to ' *go on to perfection.*' The more explicitly and strongly you
press all believers to aspire after *full sanctification*
as *attainable now by simple faith*, the more the
whole work of God will prosper." (Vol. VII.,
page 184.)

1786.

" I have not for many years known this society

in so prosperous a condition.   This is undoubtedly owing first to the exact discipline which has for
some time been observed among them; and next
to the strongly and continually exhorting believers
to ' *go on to perfection*.' "   (Journal.)

1787.

" It requires a great degree of watchfulness to
retain the perfect love of God; and one great
means of retaining it is frankly to declare what
God has given you, and earnestly to exhort all the
believers you meet to follow after full salvation."
(Vol. VII., page 13.)

1789.

" I am glad to find that your love does not grow
cold; nor your desires after all the mind that was
in Christ.   O, be satisfied with nothing less;
and you will receive it by simple faith."   (Vol.
VII., page 124.)

"About one I preached to another very serious
congregation in the town; whom therefore I exhorted to leave the first principles and go on to
perfection."   (Vol. IV., page 732.)

1790.

" I am glad that Brother D—— has more light
with regard to *full sanctification*.   This doctrine
is the grand *depositum* which God has lodged

with the people called Methodists; and for the
sake of propagating this chiefly he appears to
have raised us up." (Vol. VII., page 153.)

Who was it said that Mr. Wesley had changed
his views in 1784?

" To retain the grace of God is much more
than to gain it; hardly one in three does this.
And this should be strongly and explicitly urged
on all who have tasted of *perfect love*. If we can
prove that any of our local preachers or leaders,
either directly or indirectly, speak against it, let
him be a local preacher or leader no longer. I
doubt whether he should continue in the society;
because he that could speak thus in our congregation cannot be an honest man." (Letter to Dr.
A. Clarke, Vol. VII., page 206.)

Shades of Wesley! What would he think to-
day if he saw his preachers turned out of pulpits,
and located, discounted, and ridiculed for believing in, obtaining, and preaching this very grace
and experience which he says Methodists were
chiefly raised up to propagate? He actually says
that if any of the preachers or leaders speak
against it he should be a preacher or leader no
longer, and doubts whether he should continue
in the society! If Mr. Wesley were here to-day,

what a tremendous change and revolution in Church affairs there would be!

1791.

"A man that is not a thorough friend to Christian perfection will easily puzzle others, and thereby weaken, if not destroy, any select society." (Vol. VII., page 238.)

Here is given the explanation of how a great Holiness church, full of fire, can go down under the pastorate of a man who secretly opposes or openly fights the doctrine and experience that gave the Church its power and made it such a wonderful success. Mr. Wesley says that such a course "puzzles," "weakens," and "destroys" any "select society." Some of the brethren to-day say that the church went down because there was nothing in it, that the whole thing was a soap bubble; Mr. Wesley says that it goes down by a man opposing the doctrine of Christian perfection.

"Whenever you have opportunity of speaking to believers, urge them to go on to perfection. Spare no pains! And God, even our own God, still give you his blessing." (Vol. VII., page 238.)

More extracts and quotations could be given; one six weeks before he died, and another three

4

days before his spirit passed away. But enough has been written to show that Mr. Wesley never changed his views; but died as he lived, a firm believer in a second work of grace and blessing for believers, which he calls perfection or full sanctification, and which he steadily insisted on was obtainable now by simple faith.

CHAPTER VI.

BIBLE PROOF OF INBRED SIN.

The Two Sin Offerings—The Twofold Presentation of the
Blood—The Fountain of Cleansing—The Purging
Fire—"The Stony Heart."

SOME writers have said that, while there is no
verse or passage of Scripture that teaches by
direct statement a second work of grace, yet that
the books of the New Testament are written in
recognition of such a work; and, taken as a
whole, are an exhortation to the believer to press
on and obtain the grace.

We believe that the second work is taught in
both ways: laid down in a general way, as just
mentioned, but also taught specifically in verse
and passage.

In like manner inbred sin is taught in both
ways. It is shown up in the different books of the
Bible by a recognition and admission of the evil,
and by exhortations and directions in regard to its
removal.

We marvel that a man can read the New Testament and not see the distinct recognition of the

evil nature left in the believer, and be impressed
with the urgent appeals and commands to press
on to a certain and blessed deliverance.

No goal was ever plainer before the eyes of the
racer than the possibility of the obtainment of purity and perfect love in this life is made to shine
before the gaze of the regenerated man.

With these prefatory remarks, let us see where
we can find the "remainder of iniquity" taught
in the Bible.

Inbred sin is first recognized in the Levitical
rites of the Old Testament, in the requirement of
two different kinds of animals in the sacrifice for
sin—viz., the bullock and the goat. The goat is a
coarser and ranker animal than the bullock. In
this way God is pleased to call attention to and illustrate a deeper, darker, ranker nature of sin than
is seen in the life of personal transgression. There
is a stratum of evil underlying one's actual sins,
concerning the existence of which the man is again
and again admonished in his own consciousness.
The bullock stands for personal sins and guilt;
the goat represents that darker something called
depravity or original sin.

Again inbred sin is recognized in the twofold
presentation of "the blood."

Let the reader turn to Leviticus v. 9, and ask
why is it that part of the blood of the sacrifice was
poured out at the side of the altar and part at the
bottom of the altar?   The verse quoted reads:
"And he shall sprinkle of the blood of the sin
offering upon the side of the altar; and the rest
of the blood shall be wrung out at the bottom of
the altar; it is a sin offering."   All this is significant, and means what countless millions have
found out in their experience: that the blood of
Christ is presented and used twice for the full
cleansing of the soul.

Let the reader also note this truth taught again
by observing that the priest entered the Holy Place
with blood, and when once a year he entered the
Holy of Holies beyond the veil, he had to go back
to the altar and get *blood again and fire!*   Here
was a twofold presentation of the typical blood
in the tabernacle or temple, one in the outer and
the other in the inner sanctuary.

What is all this but the truth shadowed forth
that the blood of Christ is needed and has to be
offered or appropriated twice? It was in the Holy
of Holies that the second presentation of the blood
took place, and then and there the coals of fire
brought in at the same time.   It is when the blood

of Christ is trusted for the second work of purifying or sanctifying that we get the fire upon the
soul.

Inbred sin is recognized again in the double
work done by the fountain opened up in the house
of David, as described by Zechariah xiii. 1: " In
that day there shall be a fountain opened to the
house of David and to the inhabitants of Jerusalem for sin *and* for uncleanness."

The word "and," which we have Italicized, is a
copulative conjunction, and means that something
else is done. The fountain of Christ's blood does
a double work. It cleanses our personal sins, and
it can remove the uncleanness of an inherited depravity. This uncleanness is felt to be left in every
converted man, manifesting itself in thoughts, desires, imaginations, inclinations, selfishness, irritability, intolerance, and in many other ways.

Again inbred sin is taught clearly in the experience of Isaiah.

In the first eight verses of the sixth chapter of
the book called by his name, nothing could be
clearer. Isaiah at the time was the prophet of
God, and while in the temple God revealed the
heart-plague in him, which Isaiah called " uncleanness," but God termed " sin " and " iniquity."

That it was not personal transgression is seen in the declaration that it was "purged" and "taken away." Personal sins have to be forgiven, and the soul is cleansed by the washing of regeneration; but inbred sin is purged away by the baptism of fire, which was the very element God used in this case. The coal of fire from the altar touched him, the flame flew through him, and the thrilling announcement of deliverance was instantly made: "Lo, thine iniquity is taken away, and thy sin purged."

Inbred sin appears again in Ezekiel xxxvi. 26: "I will take away the stony heart out of your flesh."

Let the reader turn to this passage and read the entire paragraph, verses 23–28. Several things will at once impress the thoughtful mind; one is that the prophet was not speaking of regeneration at all, but describing a blessing that God was going to give his people in the future. There has not been a time that men have not been justified and regenerated. The patriarchs and prophets were men of God. Ezekiel himself was a servant of the Lord of the profoundest spirituality, as can be seen in his writings. Yet here he is speaking of a great coming blessing.

The twenty-third verse shows conclusively that

not regeneration but sanctification was in the mind of the prophet when he spoke of the cleansing from all filthiness, and the removal of the stony heart. The verse reads: "And the heathen shall know that I am the Lord, saith the Lord God, when I shall be sanctified in you before their eyes." This is the trouble to-day in regard to the mission work, the Church before the eyes of the heathen is not sanctified. The reason that God does not project us in great bodies into the heart of Asia and Africa is that we are not sanctified, and he does not want the heathen to see the feeble type of piety we possess. It is well known how our type of Christianity impressed the visiting Asiatics during the late great Exposition.

Besides this the very terms used in the passage, " all filthiness " cleansed, " all idols " taken out, all show that regeneration is not spoken of; for Paul distinctly says that filthiness of flesh and spirit is left in the regenerated; and we all recognize plainly in the converted man the idols of family, self, reputation, position, ambition, etc.

The crowning proof is seen in the expression, " stony heart." This is felt to be left in the regenerated. There is a universal witness to this.

What is meant by the stony heart? The Bible,

of course, does not teach that there is an actual rock in the breast, but is speaking figuratively. A stone is something cold, hard, and heavy. Has the converted man at times a cold, hard, heavy feeling in his soul? Who will dare to deny it?

It is not felt all the time. Some days the heart is light, tender, and warm. But suddenly, and at the most unexpected and undesirable of times, the stone is felt inside. The very gladness of others may bring it about. It is realized under some proposition from the pulpit. It leaps into being while kneeling at the altar. It has been strangely observed at the communion table just when one wanted to feel deeply. It arises at other times in the breast without any known cause.

A leading member and steward of a large city church said once to the author: "Your sermon greatly touched me, but when you invited us to the altar my heart turned as cold as a stone!" O, the stony heart!

One of the most prominent women in a Kentucky city withstood the power of a great revival meeting for eight days, but on the ninth day she flung herself at the altar with a loud, bitter cry that those who heard it will never forget: "O, my God! take out of me this stony heart!"

The regenerated man who reads these lines knows that he has that stony heart. Child of God as he is, yet a hard nature is left in him or his own consciousness, and the experience of the Christian world amounts to nothing.

Ezekiel says that there is a blessed work of grace in which that " stony heart " shall be taken out. If God's children still feel it remaining, then is there a blessing to be had that they have not yet obtained; for the prophet says that it shall be taken out.

Notice that the stony heart is to be " taken out," not suppressed or kept under. If taken out, we will certainly know it. Observe also that it is God who removes the trouble from the soul; not growth, not death, not purgatory. Listen! it is God speaking: " *I* will take away the stony heart out of your flesh."

CHAPTER VII.

BIBLE PROOF OF INBRED SIN (CONTINUED).

"Bent to Backsliding"—The Saviour's Words—The Baptism of the Holy Ghost.

THE deeper we go in the Bible the more specific and clear is seen the teaching in regard to inbred sin.

In Hosea xi. 7 we see it appear in the words, "And my people are *bent to backsliding* from me."

God's people are not one kind of people in one age and country and another kind in a different time and place. Regeneration is the same the world round. The wax may be different, but the signet is the same; and we recognize the stamp of the Divine Hand in all nations, conditions, and grades. His people are his people everywhere. His children are not the devil's servants. The verse above is the word of the Lord himself, and he says " my people." This settles the fact of the relation.

But about them he adds the fact that they are " bent to backsliding." O, that " bent " in the heart! It has been in the race since the fall.

God's people suffered with it in Hosea's time, and they are afflicted with it in these present times. It is confessed in private and public prayer, acknowledged in the pulpit, and sung lustily from the hymn book in the well remembered lines:

Prone to wander, Lord, I feel it.

The point that we would make is that if there is a " bent to backsliding " in God's people, that bent shows a radical trouble. If a man is " bent " upon leaving his wife, there is faithlessness, disloyalty, or lack of affection in him. To confess that we feel prone to leave the God we love is to admit an inward weakness; graver still, a trouble; deeper still, a plague of the heart that needs attention and prompt relief. This " bent," or " proneness," is not, as the Dean of a certain theological school calls it, " a liability to sin." The liability to sin is something inseparably connected with one's probationary state as a free spirit working out salvation. To pray for deliverance from liability to sin is to pray away one's moral freedom, and brings the man down to a moral machine or automaton.

A young preacher, commenting on the Dean's utterance, said he feared that the Professor's " liabilities were greater than his assets."

Be this as it may, this " bent," or " proneness,"
is felt to be far greater than a " liability to sin."
It is certainly one thing to be liable to sin, and
a totally different thing, and a far graver matter,
to feel bent to backsliding or prone to wander
from the Lord.

Christ has not come to destroy in this life the
liability or possibility of sinning, but to take out
the bent to sinning. The power to sin, or moral
freedom, adheres to the spirit as the work of
God; the proneness to sin is the work of the
devil; and this last, and not the first, is what the
Saviour has come to destroy.

It is this last thing which is felt stirring in the
regenerated heart. It is this which Christ is willing and able to remove.

> Take away the bent to sinning,
> Alpha and Omega be.

Again, inbred sin is taught in the Saviour's
words.

What solemn things he used to utter about the
heart! He described a nature lying away back and
down in us that explained the cause of all the transgressions in the world. " Out of the heart proceed evil thoughts, murders, adulteries, fornica-
tions, thefts, false witness, blasphemies." One

feels like he had looked over into a dark pit as he reads these words.

Should some one insist that all these things are removed in regeneration, we reply: Yes; these actions cease, or should cease, with the converting grace of God. But we press this question on the regenerated man as to whether he has had anger or lust in his heart since his conversion. If he has, Christ says that he has murdered and committed adultery in his heart. What a heart!

But there is another heart which Christ calls a *pure* heart. Blessed is the man who has it, says the Saviour. That man certainly has read the Bible with but little attention not to observe as taught there the difference between a new heart and a pure heart. A new heart that comes in re-generation has inbred sin in it, but under the bap-tism of fire it is purged and becomes a pure heart.

But we go on farther with the Saviour's words. On a certain occasion James and John wanted to call down fire upon a town and burn it up, be-cause it had shut its gates against them. Christ's words to them are most significant: "Ye know not what spirit ye are of." That they were his disciples and followers, and "not of the world," the Book clearly states, and yet he attributes to

them a spirit dark and the opposite of his own—
just exactly what we all found out in the regenerated life. We heard a minister preach a capital
sermon, and then afterwards say that he would have
his revenge on a fellow-minister for a wrong, real or
imaginary. There was a " spirit in him " evidently not of Christ. It was not a temptation; it was
something *in him*.

Does the reader recall how the Saviour on a certain occasion said to Peter, " Get thee behind me,
Satan?" If it had been the devil in Peter, Christ
would not have added, " *Thou* art an offense unto
me;" but would have rebuked Satan, and said,
" Come out of him." But the word was " *Thou*
art an offense "—" thou savorest not the things
that be of God, but the things that be of men."
The depravity caused by the devil, and found
among men, was here lifting itself up in the band
of the apostles in the presence of the Saviour
himself. Christ called it Satan, and well he did,
for inbred sin is the work of Satan; and here this
work was manifesting itself in one of his own disciples.

Inbred sin is taught again in the baptism of the
Holy Ghost.

Many have regarded the marvelous work of the

Son of God in baptizing the soul with fire as simply a filling and empowering for service. As a doctrine it is without any offense to the world or Church if presented and sought as an enduement of power or qualification for Christian work. It is only when the other hemisphere of the truth is held up that we hear at once the protest and feel the resistance.

This other hemisphere or part of the work is the *purification* of the heart. The baptism with the Holy Ghost by the Son of God does two things: it purifies the heart and empowers for service. Purifying, filling, abiding, is the order. The Holy Ghost becomes a constant indweller. " He shall abide with you forever."

The Saviour spoke clearly of the *empowering* through the evangelist Luke in Acts i. 8, " Ye shall receive *power* after that the Holy Ghost is come upon you;" while the Holy Ghost himself inspired Peter to speak of the *purifying* in Acts xv. 8, 9, "And God, which knoweth the hearts, bare them witness, *giving them the Holy Ghost even as he did unto us;* and put no difference between us and them, *purifying* their hearts by faith."

Here the apostle identifies the blessing that came

upon Cornelius with that which the disciples received at Pentecost.   He said that there was " no
difference," and that their hearts were purified at
that time.

The disciples previous to Pentecost were Christ's
followers, were preachers, had cast out devils, had
their names written in the Book of Life, and according to the Saviour in his prayer in the seventeenth chapter of John " were not of the world; "
and yet on the morning of Pentecost their hearts
were " purified."

If their hearts were purified that day, then there
was *impurity* beforehand.   And this is what we
contend is taught by the Bible and verified in human experience: that there is impurity, a remainder of iniquity left in the regenerated man; that a
pardoned soul is one thing, and a purified soul another thing altogether.

Moreover, the purifying is taught in the term
" fire."   " He will baptize you with fire! "   What
for, pray?   What does fire do?

Every one knows that fire is destructive and purifying.   There is no other agent on earth that is
more destructive and so purifying.

The Lord knew that we would remember this,
and that when he promised a baptism of fire upon
	5

the soul we would straightway see that there was
something to destroy in the soul, a nature to purify.

According to the consciousness of the soul this
is what takes place in the baptism of the Holy
Ghost.   Whoever receives it feels that a troublesome something has been taken out of him, and
that the earth has suddenly become very beautiful.   Heaven has come down to us—yes, in us—
through the possession of a pure heart.

God has undoubtedly taught the fact of remaining corruption in the regenerated, protecting the
doctrine of a second work of grace in the symbol
of fire.

The fires of earth destroy and purify; the fire
that Christ sends down upon the soul likewise destroys and purifies.   Here is a figure that in itself
alone defends the truth from all enemies, from Zinzendorf down to the latest writer in the church.   It
is the Gibraltar against which the waves of controversy and denial must lash and pound in vain.

CHAPTER VIII.

The "Old Man"—The "Flesh."

INBRED sin appears again in Ephesians iv. 22:
"That ye put off concerning the former conversation the old man, which is corrupt according to
the deceitful lusts."

Here is an exhortation not to sinners, but to a
church. Certain expressions in this Epistle show
beyond all question the spiritual condition of the
members of the church. Paul says that they were
"quickened" who had been "dead in trespasses
and in sins;" that they were once "afar off,"
but were now "made nigh by the blood of Christ;"
that they were no more strangers and foreigners,
but "fellow-citizens with the saints and of the
household of God." Still again he tells them to
forgive one another "even as God for Christ's
sake hath forgiven you," and a few verses after
that states: "Ye were sometime darkness, but
now are ye light in the Lord: walk as children
of light."

These expressions undoubtedly declare the saved condition of the people to whom the apostle wrote. And yet to these who were "forgiven" and "light in the Lord" and "of the household of God" he writes: "Put off the old man."

Could anything be plainer? Does not the reader see that something dark and evil is left in the heart of the regenerated man? That this something which is here called the "old man" is not to be pardoned, but taken away, put off, removed.

If this were the only verse in the Bible that taught inbred sin, it would be a Gibraltar for the doctrine.

Let not the reader be confused by the following verse, "and be renewed in the spirit of your mind," thinking that this is regeneration. Let him turn to Romans xii. 2, where Paul exhorts the *brethren* to this very grace in which they will be "transformed by the renewing of your mind." Here evidently the "renewing" is not regeneration, for the people he exhorts are "brethren" and "living sacrifices" already.

Still more light thrown on the words "renew" and "renewing" as used in these connections, is obtained in Titus iii. 5: "He saved us by the washing of regeneration, *and* the *renewing* of the

Holy Ghost; which he *shed* on us abundantly
through Jesus Christ our Saviour.'' The Italicized
words will open the eyes. Salvation is seen to
be a double work, and the last work comes with
the baptism of the Holy Ghost and fire. When
it came the Apostle Peter said in Acts ii. 33: '' He
shed forth this, which ye now see and hear.''

Regeneration is a birth, and not a shedding forth.
The baptism of the Holy Ghost was '' shed forth ''
according to Peter. This additional work Paul
had in mind when he wrote to Titus as quoted
above, mentioning the two works and calling the
second '' the renewing of the Holy Ghost.''

The mistake made by many is in making these
words '' renew,'' '' renewed,'' '' renewing,'' refer every time to regeneration. The expression
'' new creature'' always refers to the regenerated
man, but the words '' renewing of the Holy
Ghost '' evidently stand for a subsequent work.
Let the reader turn to Titus iii. 5 again: ''He saved
us, by the washing of regeneration, *and* renewing of the Holy Ghost, which he *shed* on us abundantly through Jesus Christ our Saviour.'' The
word '' and,'' which we have Italicized, is a copulative conjunction, and always means something
else in addition to what went before.

In full confirmation of the thought advanced we read in Ephesians iv. 24 that immediately after Paul says the "old man" must be " put off" he adds: "And that ye put on the new man, which after God is created in righteousness and *true holiness.*" Here is taught the coming upon us and in us of Christ which follows instantly the removal of inbred sin or putting off the "old man."

Let no one make the mistake of thinking that this is the first coming of Christ to the soul. As he cleansed the temple twice, he has a second cleansing for the soul. This last purifies from inbred sin. The "old man" is cast out; and Christ, the New Man, will come now not as a visitor, but as a perpetual indweller. This is what he promised in John xiv. 23 to his disciples and all else of his followers who will love him and keep his words: " We will come unto him, and make our abode with him." This is the " mystery which hath been hid from ages and from generations, but now is made manifest to his saints; . . . which is Christ *in* you."

Regenerated people are termed " saints " in the Epistles; and here Paul says is a mystery long hid, but now revealed to them, " Christ in you." For this same thing he " travails in birth again " for

the Galatians that Christ might be formed in them
" the hope of glory."

The New Man will *visit* the regenerated heart,
and sweet and delightful are these visits; but
he will not take up his *abode* with inbred sin.
Hence the regenerated man is constantly made
to wonder and grieve over the absence of Christ
from the soul. He went to bed happy with
his presence, but awoke, and the Saviour was
gone. All this was Christ's way of showing that
he will not *abide* in the heart with unsurrendered
and unexpelled inbred sin. This very departure
of his lightsome and joyous presence without sin
having been committed was intended of him to
occasion deep searchings for the cause, and the
discovery of carnality or the remainder of iniquity.

The instant the "old man" is "put off" Paul
says that we "put on" the New Man. Christ enters the heart to stay. He ceases to be a visitor,
and becomes an indweller and abider.

Still again inbred sin is seen in Galatians v. 17:
" For the flesh lusteth against the Spirit, and the
Spirit against the flesh: and these are contrary the
one to the other; so that ye cannot do the things
that ye would."

Here inbred sin is called the "flesh."

Notice that a church is being written to. This time it is a church that has gotten into bondage; just such a bondage as we see many churches and Christian individuals in to-day. "O foolish Galatians, who hath bewitched you? . . . Having begun in the Spirit, are ye now made perfect by the flesh?"

They had become entangled by the vain hope and endeavor to reach perfection by the deeds of the law. "This only would I learn of you," said Paul: "Received ye the Spirit by the works of the law, or by the hearing of faith?" And in the fourteenth verse he continues, calling attention to Abraham's faith: "That we might receive *the promise of the Spirit through faith.*"

Does not any Bible student know that "the promise of the Spirit" is not regeneration, but that which Christ told regenerated disciples to tarry for in Jerusalem until it came upon them?

All this settles the condition of the Galatian church; they had begun in the Spirit, but had made the mistake of believing that they could be made perfect by the deeds of the law, and so had gotten into bondage.

This was the explanation of their now being "removed from him that called you into the grace of Christ unto another gospel." Truly it is another gospel that teaches perfection by the deeds of the law.

Let the reader get this idea, and he has the key that unlocks the book of Galatians. They were not sinners, but had been " troubled " by teachers who had "perverted the gospel." They had gotten to observing " times and seasons," had been " hindered " in their " running well; " in a word, entangled in a yoke of bondage. That they were still the Lord's people is seen in the way that Paul addresses them, calling them " my little children " and " brethren," and saying to them, " Ye are spiritual," etc.

There is nothing said to them by way of rebuke that cannot be said to any body of Christians who seek perfection by the deeds of the law.

Now to this church Paul writes; and in the seventeenth verse of the fifth chapter describes their inward state, and for that matter the state of every regenerated man on earth in the words: " The flesh lusteth against the Spirit, and the Spirit against the flesh."

The word " flesh" does not mean the body. The word in the Greek is *sarx*, signifying the carnal mind. It has been observed that Paul

adopts the word *sarx* to describe carnality,
and the word *soma* to speak of the body. In
this instance it is *sarx*, and not *soma*.

A strong proof of this interpretation is seen in
the fact that God has no quarrel with the body;
the Spirit does not lust against the body. Sin is
not in the body, as it does not, and cannot, exist
in any form of matter. The *soma*, or body, is the
work of God; while the *sarx*, flesh or carnality, is
the work of the devil. If we get the *sarx* out, the
soma will be all right. If the "flesh" be burned
out of us by the baptism of fire, we will find the
body all right.

It is, then, the "flesh" (*sarx*) that Paul says
was left in these Galatian Christians, which lust-
ed against the Spirit, so that he wrote: "Ye cannot [may not] do the things ye would."

Let the reader note the striking fact that the
Spirit here mentioned is not the man's soul, but
the Spirit of God. The letter "S" is here a capital, and reference is made to the Holy Ghost.
So the contest going on that the apostle speaks of
is not a conflict between a man's body and soul,
but between the "flesh" and the Holy Spirit.

The point that we make is that if the "flesh,"
or carnality, was left in the Galatian church,

whom Paul calls "brethren" and "spiritual,"
then is it left in converted people in America.
And this is just what every true and honest regenerated man will admit when questioned on the
subject, whether he lives in Galatia, Europe, Africa, America, or the isles of the sea.

CHAPTER IX.

BIBLE PROOF OF INBRED SIN (CONTINUED).

"Carnal"— "Filthiness of the Spirit"—"Sin Which Besets"—
"Superfluity of Naughtiness."

IN this chapter we begin with Paul's letter to the Corinthians, and find the thing that we are looking for in the very outstart.

In 1 Corinthians iii. 3 we have the words: "For ye are yet *carnal*."

We are not left in doubt about the religious condition of the Corinthian Christians with such expressions in the first and third chapters as follows:

"The church of God which is at Corinth," "Sanctified in Christ Jesus," "Called *to be* saints," "The grace of God which is given you," "In everything ye are enriched by him," "brethren," "babes in Christ," etc.

All regenerated people are called "saints" in the Epistles. They are not, as some suppose, "*called* to be saints." The two words "to be" are in Italics to show that they are supplied. The true reading is "called saints." The ex-

pression "sanctified in Christ Jesus," as applied
to regenerated people, is perfectly correct according to the Bible and Methodist standards.   There
is a measure of holiness or sanctification in regeneration.   The doctrine that we preach is that of
entire sanctification.   Paul's prayer was: "And
the God of peace sanctify you wholly."   The
term " babes in Christ " settles the fact of the regeneration of the Corinthians.   If " babes," they
certainly must have been born of the spirit.

Now concerning these very people, Paul declares in 1 Corinthians iii. 3 the fact that they are
" carnal."   The word in the Greek is *sarki-*
koi, and means " carnality," " the flesh," or
" fleshliness."   One can easily see that it is not the
body referred to, for it would be silly to say: " Ye
have yet a body."

So regenerated Corinthians, according to the
words of inspiration, have carnality or fleshliness
in them.   Alas for Zinzendorf and his American
followers who claim that regeneration brings a
pure heart, utterly failing to distinguish between a
new and a pure heart!   They are not the same.
They are recognized as different in the Bible, and
felt to be different things in the moral consciousness.

So the regenerated Corinthians had carnality!

And so have regenerated Americans, Englishmen, Frenchmen, and every other kind of men, until they allow the Saviour to burn it out.

This is the sum of general observation, and the testimony of experience, that carnality is left in the regenerated soul.

When we feel it in ourselves, see it in others, and read these plain statements in the Word of God, how is it that men can have the assurance to stand up and deny the fact?

We come to another expression in 2 Corinthians vii. 1: "Having therefore these promises, dearly beloved, let us cleanse ourselves from all *filthiness* of the flesh and spirit, perfecting holiness in the fear of God."

The spiritual relation of these same Corinthians is still recognized in the words "dearly beloved." As a church they had done wrong things, just as we see churches doing to-day. The explanation of these same troubles and aberrations in both cases is to be found in the "filthiness of the spirit" which Paul mentions here.

So there is a "filthiness" left in regenerated people! The Bible here plainly says so. Alas for Zinzendorf and the "makers of another gospel!"

We have only to listen to the prayers of regenerated people to hear them confess to this same
filthiness within.   They deplore inward uncleanness.   They beg for clean hearts, and cannot
pray the simplest ordinary prayer without admit-
ting again and again the truth for which we are
contending in this book.

It is not a filthiness to be pardoned, but cleansed.

We are told, it is true, to " cleanse ourselves "
from this filthiness.   This at first glance would
seem to indicate that it was a personal transgression after all.   But we have only to call attention
to kindred phrases like: " Save yourselves,"
" Pray without ceasing," " Be ye holy," and others.   We know that in each instance we are called
to a state and experience that no man can bring
himself into.   No one can " save himself " nor
" pray without ceasing " without the sanctifying
grace of God, nor " be holy " until the purifying
fire of Pentecost descends.   We are called to these
states, and by complying with certain conditions
we instantly find ourselves uplifted by Divine grace
and power into the blessing itself.

So here we are to " cleanse ourselves " in the
same manner.   Who believes that a man can take
a " filthiness of spirit " out of himself?   If he

could, he would be a Saviour. But he aims repeated blows at the external manifestation of the
inward uncleanness, separates himself from every
appearance of evil, and, placing himself on the altar, believing and praying, suddenly God does
the work, and the man filled with joy feels that
the foulness is gone and he has a pure heart.

The words "perfecting holiness" show something that has not up to that time been obtained
and enjoyed. One meaning of the word "perfecting" in the original is "to bring to an end,"
"to finish," "to complete." Surely there is a
perfecting of holiness, a blessing called entire
sanctification; and when it is accomplished, we
above all others know it.

Still another recognition of inbred sin is to be
found in Hebrews xii. 1: "Lay aside every
weight, and *the sin which doth so easily beset us.*"

There is a marked difference in the Scripture
between the plural "sins" and "sin" in the singular number. Both Paul and John are very clear
in their discrimination between the two. The first
are to be forgiven, the second is to be "destroyed," "put off," "laid aside," etc.

It is sin in the singular number that "the Lamb
of God taketh away;" it is sin in the singular

number that is cleansed by the blood of Christ while we are in the light as he is in the light, and having fellowship one with another; right then while in the light the Blood cleanses away that sin of the singular number. It is that same " sin " as opposed to transgressions or " sins " that the apostle says is to be " laid aside."

What is this " sin which doth so easily beset us" that is spoken of here but inbred sin. The colored preacher was not so far wrong when he read the verse: " The sin which doth so easily *upset* us." It is the besetting sin of every child of Adam. It is in all, but cannot be forgiven. The words used to describe the manner it is dealt with are " put off," " taketh away," " laid aside " and " destroyed."

In James i. 21 we have another view of inbred sin in the words: " Wherefore lay apart all filthiness and *superfluity of naughtiness.*"

That a body of Christians is being written to is evident from the frequently recurring phrases, " brethren," " beloved brethren," and the advice given them in regard to the treatment of different classes in the house of God.

There is no rebuke, no instruction given them; but what is delivered to believers to-day in warn-

6

ings about the tongue and the way of treating the poor and rich.

To these same " beloved brethren " who have already " the engrafted word," he says: "Lay apart all superfluity of naughtiness." This expression has puzzled many, and once mystified the writer. For a long time he supposed that it referred to an abounding in wickedness. But one of the finest Greek scholars in the land informed him that if he would consult the Greek Lexicon he would discover the true meaning to be, " the remainder of iniquity," or " a residue over and above." Truly there is a remainder of iniquity, a residuum of sin.

Then here is the word " filthiness " used again. And it is to be laid apart. It is remarkable how invariably the idea of separation is impressed whenever this dark residue of sin is mentioned in the Bible. It is never to be forgiven, but the great fact of removal and separation is always taught.

If some one would say that the filthiness here may be questionable practices and habits, that we see regenerated people at times drifting into; then the other expression "superfluity of naughtiness" or the remainder of iniquity still remains to show up the fact of inbred sin.

CHAPTER X.

"The Double Mind."

INBRED sin is seen again in James iv. 8: "Purify your hearts, ye double-minded."

The apostle is writing to Christians, as we have shown in the foregoing chapter by the terms "brethren," "beloved brethren," and other expressions still more striking where the Word is said to be "engrafted," and that they have been "begotten by the Word."

It is true that the apostle indulges in some strong terms of rebuke, that if taken as a true description of the people rebuked, would seem incompatible with the Christian life, and that instead here would be not a Church, but a body of great sinners that James was after. But a little study brings light, and saves us from this mistake.

For instance, the word "curse," found in chapter iii. 9, 10, means in the original "scold." The "lusts" that he speaks of is translated in the margin "pleasures." The adultery that he inveighs against in chapter iv. 4 is, as he explains himself, "the friendship of the world."

(83)

About these very things God's people have to
be warned from the pulpit to-day. We all know
many excellent Church people who "scold," in-
dulge in "pleasures" not spiritual, and who seem
to have a decided friendliness to the world. They
are to be found on boards of stewards, and a
good many other Boards. They lead in good
works in the Church, and they lead in works that
are not so good. They entertain the bishops and
other prominent personages at Conference. They
are regarded as leading people in the Church, and
have great influence in high quarters. What
James said nearly two thousand years ago to people in the Church could be said to many to-day.

This is not all, for even now in our times we
have only to look to see the different treatment
paid in Church to the brother of low degree, and
to the man with "gay apparel" and with a "gold
ring." It is curious to notice the sensation even
among preachers and the rising up and offering of
chairs to a man of wealth or authority who comes
in late and disturbs scores of people by his late
coming. The author has seen not less than four
chairs offered to one of these prominent late
comers; while the spectacle of four or five men in
front all beckoning at once to some unseen man in

the rear of the house is a sight never to be forgotten, while it throws a strong side light on James ii. 3, where he says: "Ye have respect to him that weareth the gay clothing, and say unto him, Sit thou here in a good place."

A newspaper reporter in one of our largest cities disguised himself, and on two Sabbaths tested the sentiment of a number of the Churches in regard to the humble and poor, by presenting himself to the ushers in very plain attire. The report of his experience in various of these prominent Churches made very interesting reading. At some he was received with kindness, but at others he was plainly shown that he was not wanted. One usher kept him standing at the foot of the aisle in doubt as to whether he would give him a seat or not, when suddenly a young couple richly dressed appeared on the scene. Immediately the usher became a vision of smiles and was transformed into a bundle of springs as he escorted the gorgeous pair to a front seat. But the instant he returned to that problem in plain attire at the foot of the aisle his brow became cloudy. He had begun to resume his scrutiny of the apparent tramp, when the disguised reporter said to him that he believed he would not take a seat, but had concluded to go to the hospital. Whereupon the usher with great cordiality told him that he thought that was the best place for him. All this happened in a leading Church in one of our greatest cities.

In a word, the Epistle of James is not out of date, and its incisive utterances are still needed in the Churches. There is not a thing denounced by James in his Epistle but the author of this book has seen in the Churches of our day and country.

Yet these people were " brethren " and " beloved brethren " and had been " begotten by the Word," and the Word was " engrafted " in them.

The trouble in their case was that the double mind was left.

Who is the double-minded man? We all know who the single-minded man is. Every sinner is single-minded. He has but one mind, and that is to do wrong. There is no desire to please God. He is a unit in the endeavor to please himself and do wrong.

But under the preaching of the word he becomes convicted, is converted, has the mind of Christ imparted to him, and from that moment becomes a two-minded man.

Every regenerated man has the double mind. We do not mean anything offensive here. We do not say that he is a hypocrite, but there are two minds in him, and he himself recognizes and deplores the fact of two forces, laws, or minds warring in him, the one spiritual and the other carnal.

If he would come to God according to divine direction, the Lord would sanctify him, and take or burn out the carnal mind; and leave him with the one mind, that of Christ, and so he would become single-minded for God, as he had once been for sin and Satan. But he, for various reasons, will not come; and so has in him the consciousness, regenerated as he is, of the evil residue, the besetment, the remainder of iniquity, the flesh, the old man, or the double mind. Many regenerated people keep this double-mindedness down, and live very beautiful lives. Others grow heartsick and discouraged over the frequent internal strife and uprisings, and finally almost cease to struggle against it. So we see some converted people drifting into just such lives as brought out the sharp reprimands of James upon the Church in the first century.

The feeling with many is that this dark something can never be taken out; and so, in despair, such individuals sink into a gross form of religious living, thinking that the only Saviour for

them is death. Such people finally accept a
kind of double life, and know what it is to have
two tongues and two faces. In leaving the house
in the morning they first take off the home face
and hang it up on a nail behind the hall door, and
at the same time put on the street face; and, after fitting it, sally forth. What pleasant manners
and smiles now are seen as they pass down the
street with greetings, bows, and nice speeches to
all whom they meet. After some hours they return; and on getting inside the hall door they remove the street face, hang it up on a nail, take
down the home face; and, directing the scowling
look down the hall, cry out, "Isn't dinner ready
yet?" with an angry intonation that brings the
stony look up into the wife's face, and causes the
children to glide away into distant corners.

There are less offensive manifestations of the
double mind, but they are not the less convincing.
What makes the regenerated man say that he is
"glad to see you" when in his heart he is not?
How can we reconcile the cordial greeting ex-
tended to the incoming visitor, "Well, it has been
an age since you were here," with the remark
made to a member of the family after the party
is gone, "I hope that she will never come

again; what a bore?" If this is not a double mind, then what is it?

Here are several ladies rocking together in the parlor of one of the group. One of these ladies knows that she ought to leave, that husband and children are expecting her, that home duties await her; yet still she lingers, rocking. Why this tarrying? Because she dreads the rising up of the *other mind* of her friends after she has gone. She knows that they are going to "jump on her" as soon as she leaves, and she does not want them to do it. She is well pleased with the present mind turned upon her, but it is the other mind that she dreads, and which she knows will begin operating the instant that she leaves. And yet all these ladies belong to the same church, and all are members of the Ladies' Aid Society.

Here are eight or ten preachers at Conference in a conversational ring. As they talk they punch their walking sticks or umbrellas into the soft ground. Now and then a big guffaw breaks forth. It is growing late, and it is time for them to go to their boarding places, that they may return to evening service; but each one shows a reluctance to leave the talking, laughing circle. What is the matter?

The answer is, they dread the double mind in
each other. While they are all good and true
men, they secretly fear each others' tongues.
They do not want to be criticised and discussed
by the brethren who are now so hearty and cordial. They do not want the double mind to be
turned on them in fault-finding and judgment of
the work done on circuit or district. Each one
of the ring wants to leave; but if he does, the others will tell how he failed on the station, or that
he was not the financier or revivalist or pastor that
was expected, or that he does not make a good
presiding elder, etc.

Truly there is not the slightest difficulty in finding proofs of the double mind in the regenerated
man. It is almost equal to the discovery of two
men in the individual in the two ways of looking,
talking, and acting.

Who has not seen the mirth quickly suppressed
at the approach of the unconscious victim that has
been conversationally impaled in his absence?
Who believes the blessed Christ would do such a
thing? If a Christian is guilty here, then is there
another mind and spirit in the Christian that is not
of Jesus, and we are brought face to face with
the double mind.

A preacher visited another in his private room
at a hotel during a gracious revival on the holiness
line.   He knelt down and asked the brother upon
whom he called to pray for him, and wept through
the entire prayer.   He said he wanted the blessing
of entire sanctification.   A few months afterwards
this same man, in a preachers' meeting composed
of men unfriendly to the doctrine of a second
work of grace, put himself promptly in line with
them and ridiculed without mercy the preacher
whom he had requested to pray for him, that he
might secure the blessing.

" Purify your hearts, ye double-minded."

A prominent minister in the Church wrote a com-
mendation of a certain book written by a preacher.
He said in the puff that " it was the best book of
the kind that had been written in the last ten
years."   Here comes now the point: there had
been no book of *that kind* published in ten years!

The preacher went off quite exhilarated with
the notice, and the prominent minister chuckled
with his family and friends about the adroit sentence.   The adroit sentence was simply the outcropping of the double mind!   The day came
when the preacher found out the secret sarcasm:
and so, as Revelation says, the little book that was

first like honey to the taste became afterwards
quite bitter.

But what shall we say more? Time would fail
to tell of the Judge and Doctor and Colonel and
Major and all the other living proofs and illustrations in the land of the double mind.

It is here in our midst, alas for it! But it can
be taken out by divine power. Thank God for
that! So we live and breathe and hope again.

CHAPTER XI.

The Seventh Chapter of Romans.

THE instant we mention this chapter in connection with inbred sin there is a quick and sometimes angry protest upon the part of many.

We are promptly informed that the troubled individual in this chapter is a Jew convicted under the law, and, finding it powerless to deliver him, he is correspondingly miserable.

The reply to this is that the Bible is not of private or class interpretation, and to confine this chapter to the description of the spiritual exercises of one of the smallest nations under the sun, while all the rest of the world are called on simply to look in on this moral arena and see the struggles and death conflict, is stretching the matter too far and making too great a demand on our credulity.

The effort to make the groaning person in this chapter a convicted legalist of any country and time fails as signally as the others.

A legalist, no matter who he is or where he is, is nothing but an unpardoned, unregenerated sinner. His condition is bound to be one of spiritual death, for God says he is dead in trespasses and sins.

But the man in the seventh chapter of Romans is not spiritually dead by any means. He has a law of life and good in him, while a sinner is a lawless man, and until regeneration, can have no law of good in him.

A still more remarkable proof of this person in the seventh chapter not being a legalist, and the clearest proof that he is instead, a spiritual man, is seen in the 22d verse, where he cries out: "I *delight* in the law of God after the inner man." Let the reader trace the word "delight" back into the Greek, and he will find the other meanings to be "please," "gratify," "enjoy," and "rejoice." Could an unconverted man say: "I enjoy and rejoice in the law of God?"

No unregenerated man—and a legalist or moralist is unregenerated—can *delight* in the law of God. The sinner stands in fear and awe of the divine commandments, but delight can only be felt by the spiritual man. We need only appeal to every man's memory of the sinful past! We trembled and were troubled at the law, but did not and could not feel delight.

The verse adds: "After the inner man." The sinner has no inner man. God says that he is dead in trespasses and sins. The inner man is the divine creation. How can God say that a man is dead in sin, and then add that " he delights in the law of God after the inner man?" Here would be a most palpable contradiction.

In still further proof of the regenerated state of the man of the seventh chapter, we quote the 25th verse: "So with the mind I myself serve the law of God." Does any one believe that an unpardoned man serves the law, either in his mind or anywhere else? This man in the chapter " consents unto the law that it is good," serves it with his mind, and even delights in it. He that consents to—serves and delights in—the law of God is a saved man!

Let the reader divest himself of prejudice and read the seventh chapter of Romans carefully, thoughtfully, and prayerfully, and he will see that here is no confession of a common transgressor. Here is no outrageous violator of God's commandments brought to repentance, confession, and judgment.

We fail to see a sign of repentance in the chapter. It is not justification nor pardon that the man is alluding to or begging for. He is in an agony over a dark indwelling something which keeps him from doing what he wants to do. In a word, it is the regenerated man under conviction for inbred sin.

It is wonderful how this chapter finds an echo in every converted heart, while the unregenerated man would never go to it for a picture of his condition and life.

It is also wonderful how preachers bring this chapter into their prayers; while the Episcopal Church, Sabbath after Sabbath, as a body of Christian believers, groan forth in their Litany, " We have done those things which we ought not to have done, and have left undone those things which we ought to have done!" a lamentation almost entirely taken from the 15th verse of the seventh chapter, " What I would, that do I not; but what I hate, that do I; " and in the 19th verse, " the good that I would, I do not; but the evil which I would not, that I do."

Another Church is very fond of quoting a part of the 24th verse, " O wretched man that I am! who shall deliver me from the body of this death?" They quote it as if it were the utterance of despair, and as if there were no deliverance mentioned immediately afterwards.

Is it not strange that, if this chapter be the experience of a convicted legalist, preachers and Churches should be adopting its language as expressive and descriptive of their own condition! Here verily is a proof in itself that it is a portrayal of the Christian conflict before the deliverance of inbred sin takes place in the glorious blessing of sanctification.

The Church might as well come to it. The battle has already started on this chapter, and we see nothing but victory for the cause of holiness in what will transpire in the probing study and honest application of this chapter.

But very earnest objections are filed against us for construing the seventh chapter as being the conviction for and the struggle of the regenerated man against inbred sin.

One objection urged is that this man here confesses that he is " carnal."

The reply to this is: Yes, but did not Paul say that the Corinthians, who were " babes in Christ," and hence born of God, were carnal? This is the very point that we are making in this book: that carnality, or the carnal mind, is left in the regenerated heart.

A second objection is that the person talking here says that he is " sold under sin."

7

This is true, but he did not say that he was sinning as a common transgressor. He said he was " *sold* under sin," and as a certain famous Holiness evangelist said, " Satan sold Adam and the whole human race out for a mess of apples." Sinning is one thing, " sold under sin " is another. We find ourselves in this world with a sinful nature which comes to us by an act of our federal head in the garden of Eden where he exchanged obedience to God for fleshly gratification. He made a bad trade; in fact, he sold the human race for something pleasing to the eye and taste.

Now let us turn from these objections and see what this man of the seventh chapter of Romans is troubled about. In trying to do this, the other objections that are urged against our interpretation will be answered. Let us note carefully the confessions and complaints made herein.

First, " What I would, that do I not."

Let the regenerated man say if he has not had to say this a thousand times since his conversion. O the Christlikeness, the usefulness, the great and good deeds we aimed after and failed to be and do and reach in the past years!

Secondly, " But what I hate, that do I."

David said that he hated vain thoughts. The

converted man says the same. He says that he
will watch the door of his lips and keep his tongue
as with a bridle, for he hates gossip and fault-finding; but there is not a day but he slips up on the
very thing he hates. He has made a covenant with
his eyes; but somehow they look, and the trouble
is that the look is just one second too long. "O
wretched man that I am!"

Thirdly, "Evil is present with me."

Does not every man grieve over the fact? The
preacher is delivering a faithful message to his
congregation. He is doing it in humility and faith-
fulness when suddenly a voice whispers, "You
are surpassing yourself," and lo! a sudden puff of
self-inflation, a special effort put forth to increase
the approbation and admiration that are read in the
faces of the audience. "O wretched man that I
am!"

A collection is being taken up for Missions. A
brother cries out from the congregation: "Put
me down twenty-five dollars." He observes the
flutter that his gift produces—perhaps he sees the
bishop looking at him—and so he cries again:
"Put me down another twenty-five!" "O
wretched man that I am!" That last twenty-
five was not right. "Evil is present with me!"

Yes, evil is present with us, and oftentimes jumps astride a good deed and rides it a mile or so before we can get it off.

Fourthly, "I see another law in my members, warring against the law of my mind."

Look at it; here are two laws, and they are dissimilar, and they are both in the same man. Surely this is not an unregenerated man, for the sinner does not serve God at all, while this character speaks of a law of life and good, against which another law in him rebels and wars.

It is not possible to live a converted life a few hours before discovering that there are now *two* laws, where before there was only one, and that one a law of sin and death. In the sinful life the members ruled, the law of sin dominated without a rival. But when regenerated, a law of life is introduced and the battle begins. Before this Satan and sin had it all their own way; now the war commences, and a fearful one it often proves to be.

Fifthly, "Bringing me into captivity."

Who has not felt bondage in the regenerated life, both to people and circumstances? Who has not deplored the lack of freedom in prayer, testimony, preaching, and living? Something within brings us as regenerated people again and again into captivity. We do not feel free. Listen to a preacher groaning in the pulpit before he preaches. What is the matter? He does not know whether he will have *liberty* or not. Hear him groaning after the sermon; he says he was not *free*. Listen to a brother laboring in prayer. Something is holding him down. Notice the silent Christian tongue, the inactive Christian life, the melancholy Christian face, the uneasy, anxious Christian heart—what is all this but captivity?

Forced into silence, or forced into speech! Afraid to declare one's convictions! Kept from doing things that have been whispered by the Spirit and taught by the Word! Captivity! Captivity!! Captivity!!! "O wretched man that I am!"

But listen, the man in the seventh chapter is still complaining.

Sixthly, "Sin dwelleth in me."

Does not the reader see that this is no allusion to personal transgressions? "Sin" in the singular number is here used. It is not personal transgressions spoken of, but inbred sin. It is something that *dwelleth* in the man. A person can leave his sins and yet this dark, sad thing remain in the heart. A man may not be in " sins " and yet the " sin " spoken of above may " dwell " or be in him.

It is because people have not discriminated here between these two terms, " sins " and " sin," that they have not been able to understand 1 John i. 8: " If we say that we have no sin, we deceive ourselves." The careless reader construes this statement to mean that we are compelled to commit sins, when the allusion is to the very thing Paul is talking about in the expression, " Sin dwelleth in me," or in other words, inbred sin.

Of course a man is utterly unable to free himself of this inward plague by any strength of his own. A person might as well try to fly from his shadow, or to put an end to his shadow by stripping himself of his clothing, as to endeavor to rid himself of this indwelling evil principle by laying aside his transgressions.

We have sometimes thought that the Saviour referred to this inward nature of sin when he said to the Jews: " Your sin remaineth." Let it be remembered that it is Christ's work to destroy the works of the devil. He has come to purify the heart. John the Baptist said that He was the Lamb of God that taketh away the *sin* of the world. If

Jew or Gentile reject him, who alone can take out this " sin," then the words of the Saviour fall indeed like a funeral knell, and they are as true as they are melancholy: " Your sin remaineth!" It is idle to narrow the expression down to one deed of evil of the elders and scribes; a deeper, truer insight into the words shows the dark nature back of the Saviour's rejection, and back of all the other sins of that nation. Back of "sins" is seen—" sin!"

Some have criticised the expression, "inbred sin;" but when we hear Christ saying, " Your sin remaineth," and Paul writing, " Sin dwelleth in me," we must confess that the term " inbred sin " has a wonderfully homogeneous sound.

Moreover, we have only to listen to hear falling from regenerated lips in pulpit and in pew, in prayer, song, testimony, and sermon, the very words in the seventh chapter of Romans: "Sin [not sins] dwelleth in me."

Seventhly, " The law of sin."

Here is no confession of actual sins, but a lamentation over a " law of sin." The man in the seventh chapter finds it manifesting itself and operating in his " members," of tongue, eyes, ears, hands, feet, and body generally, through the appetites.

He calls it a "law," although it is sinful and bad. A law can be bad. We have a number in our country that are full of evil. State Legislatures and Congress passed them. So the devil, with the consent of Adam, passed a bad law or law of sin in our spiritual being, under which the human race has languished for six thousand years. As a law it has force and authority, and millions daily go down under its baleful influence. We have all felt it, and will continue to feel it, until we allow the Saviour to abrogate and destroy it with his sancti-fying power.

Eighthly, "The body of death."

Paul does not call it death, but "body of death." Many of our readers are familiar with the allusion that the apostle here makes by the "body of death." It was a mode of punishment for certain kinds of criminals in the Roman Empire. A corpse was tied face to face with the living but condemned man, and he was then put in the prison yard or cell to wait until the decomposition of the dead body struck death into himself.

It is a fearful picture; and a newly converted person, full of his first love, and not yet convicted for inbred sin, would likely protest against the ap-plication of the figure to himself. But we must remember that the man in the seventh chapter is a *convicted* regenerated man. A sinner is one thing, and a convicted sinner is another. All can see the difference. So a Christian is one thing, but a Christian who has obtained a sight of the " old man " in his heart is quite another spectacle.

When the Holy Ghost flashes his light into the soul and shows the uncleanness there, and the lack of conformity to Christ, like Isaiah the man cries out, " Woe is me! for I am undone! " and like Paul he actually writhes under the consciousness of this inward " body of death," and so groans out, " O wretched man that I am! "

The writer has seen many regenerated people enter upon a Holiness meeting with great restfulness of spirit and self-satisfaction. Sometimes they have abounded in smiles, bantering words, and lightness of manner. But as the days proceeded, and the sword of the Spirit cut down between soul and spirit and discerned the thoughts and intents of the heart, a great change came over them. They became silent, anxious, troubled, miserable, and groaned out in their testimonies and prayers all that Paul said in the seventh chapter of Romans.

There is a second conviction for the human soul.

Not a second repentance, however, for we cannot
repent for inbred sin; we are convicted for that.
The first conviction is for personal sins; the second, for inbred sin. With the writer the last was
far more painful than the first. In the first it was
" sins " that bore him down; in the second it was
" the law of sin," " the body of death," that laid
him in the dust with cries, " O wretched man that
I am ! "

This body of death is an evil nature, principle,
or bias—call it what we will—that is like death in
the presence of the regenerated soul. The converted man feels within him something that is an-
tagonistic to the spiritual life he has obtained. It
seems to have a deadly influence. It kills joy in
the heart, kills life in prayer, kills religious energy repeatedly, kills Christian faith, hope, and love
time and time again; so that there is a struggle
against this " body of death," which seems to be
sending out a cold, chilling, death-like influence
through every open avenue to the converted soul.

Not a regenerated man but has felt the burden
of death in a measure, while every *convicted* regenerated man feels the whole weight of this ghastly body and pants for deliverance.

Ninthly, " Who shall deliver me? "

The reader will observe that here is no prayer for pardon, but for deliverance. If it was personal iniquity or sins that the man had committed, the seventh chapter of Romans would have to be similar to the fifty-first Psalm, and the apostle would be pleading for forgiveness, and crying: " Blot out my transgression."

But there is no cry for pardon in the seventh chapter. The open sinner, legalist, or moralist— all alike need to beg for forgiveness; but there is no such petition here.

The entreaty is for deliverance! And not deliverance from personal sins, but from a *law* of sin, a *body* of death, a something that *dwelleth* within; and which the agonizer wanted out. All this coincides and harmonizes exactly with the expressions, "put off," "lay aside," "take away," and the still deeper terms, "crucified" and "destroyed."

Right here in this cry, " O wretched man that I am! who shall deliver me from the body of this death?" most people stop. It is the *Miserere* of many souls, the funeral dirge of hope. They utter it in despair of deliverance. They go on through life saying, " O wretched man that I am!" and failing to see that there is a deliverance and a Deliverer. Bogged down in a Slough of Despond they think that all that is left them to do is to roll and struggle and continue to cry: " O wretched man that I am ! "

They fail to see that Paul did not remain in the slough; that he caught sight of a Deliverer in the Saviour, and that the wail of sorrow is followed by a shout of joy! Listen! " O wretched man that I am! who shall deliver me from the body of this death?" Listen again—he is shouting!—"I thank God, through Jesus Christ our Lord ! ! ! "

So he is out of the slough! Out of the seventh chapter! Out on the solid bank on the other side and running and shouting down the eighth chapter of Romans! Listen to him: " I thank God! I thank God! I thank God! through Jesus Christ our Lord ! "

Yes, indeed; Christ has done it, and can do it. He is the Lamb of God that taketh away the sin of the world. He is the Lion of the Tribe of Judah, who breaks every chain. He destroys the works of the devil in us by casting out inbred sin. The Son has made us free indeed.

Still further down the road in the eighth chapter of Romans we hear Paul's voice floating back:

" There is now therefore no condemnation to them which are in Christ Jesus."

The burden is all gone. No inward groaning or sighing. Our hearts condemn us not; God condemns us not; there is *no* condemnation.

Again floats back the voice of joy: " For the law of the Spirit of life in Christ Jesus hath made me *free* from the law of sin and death."

Hallelujah! Free! And in this blessed state the soul enjoys the unclouded favor of Heaven. No sense of being brought into captivity—he is now free.

Still again we hear the voice of the enraptured apostle, and now still further up the road: " The Spirit of God beareth witness with our spirit, that we are the children of God."

What does he mean by this? Does not the Spirit bear witness in regeneration? Certainly. But all converted people know the gaps and breaks in the divine favor, the painful silences upon the part of the divine voice, that are realized from time to time to the great inward distress of the child of God. The hindrance to the unbroken testimony of the Spirit is inbred sin. Take that out, and then all the time, all the time, all the time, " The Spirit of God beareth witness with our

spirit, that we are the children of God.'' With sanctification or the elimination of inbred sin comes
the continuous witness of the Spirit to us of our
acceptance with God.

Once more we hear Paul's voice far down the
chapter, and this time we hear him saying: '' I
reckon that the sufferings of this present time are
not worthy to be compared with the glory which
shall be revealed in us.''

This is what any man will say when inbred sin
is gone, and no condemnation is felt like a weight
upon the heart, and when the Spirit is always
whispering that we are children of God—heirs
of heaven and joint heirs with Jesus Christ. '' I
reckon,'' says Paul; and so we all say. We
reckon—yes, we *know*—that the glory to be, shall
outstrip the shame and suffering that is, beyond all
words to describe. What shall we do under such
an exhilarating thought? Christ tells us. He
says: '' Leap for joy!''

Once more the apostle's voice is wafted faintly
back. It is now at the end of the chapter. He
seems to be still shouting. '' For I am persuaded,
that neither death, nor life, nor angels, nor princi-
palities, nor powers, nor things present, nor things
to come, nor height, nor depth, nor any other

creature, shall be able to separate us from the love of God, which is in Christ Jesus our Lord."

He is evidently feeling well, and is undoubtedly established. No wonder he rejoices and shouts. Just so is established the sanctified man, and so he feels comfortable all the time, " rejoices ever- more," and shouts on his way to Christ and crowns and glory and loved ones in Heaven.

CHAPTER XII.

THE dark something left in the regenerated heart God names, and names correctly. It is a pity that men do not accept the divine description, and so find out the truth. Instead, multitudes rush forward with their descriptive titles and appellations, and of course come short in recognizing the evil and presenting the deliverance.

Satan is perfectly willing that we should name this indwelling evil, for he knows that we will not name it correctly, and hence, not knowing what it is, will not proceed properly in regard to its removal, and so the trouble will remain.

Some call it "surprises into sin." One would suppose from this that sin was more alert than grace. Let us remember that, if the evil one arises early in the morning, our Saviour is the Morning Star! In fact, we are told that he comes even at midnight. Instead of sin surprising us, Christ in us can surprise sin and Satan.

Others call it "nervousness." So when these

persons jerk the horse, slam the door, kick over the chair, speak the hot, petulant word, and slap the child's face, they call it " nervousness." It is not anger, petulance, irritability, much less the outcropping of inbred sin in them. O no! it is simply a disordered condition of the nervous system, and they are in sore need of phosphates.

We have studied this class of people and found out that all the phosphates and nerve tonics on earth fail to relieve them. The disease is not in the nerves, but in the heart.

A third class call inbred sin " infirmity." We always feel like smiling when we hear the word. We seem to hear the rustle of fig leaves and behold Adam and Eve trying to cover themselves with those interesting pieces of vegetable matter. The word " infirmity " is a fig leaf to cover spiritual bareness.

A fourth class admit the existence of the evil, and bring it forth with the confession of "feeling badly." Still others say that they feel that " something is wrong " in the heart.

How inbred sin forces such confessions as these to the lips! Its very complaints and restless spirit and fault-finding tongue are enough to make one see that something is not as it should be in the
8

soul. We remember to have " felt badly " many
times in the fourteen years of our regenerated experience. The " something wrong " feeling is a
telegram from the soul that sin in some form is
inside.

A famous writer in the Zinzendorfian wing of
the Methodist Church calls inbred sin a " susceptibility to temptation." Such a definition is a reflection upon the intelligence and moral consciousness of the Christian world. For what man cannot distinguish between a mere capacity to be
tempted and a conscious inward stirring of an evil
principle that seems to be part of himself. Truly
an external pressure of evil is one thing, and an
internal weight is another. The first may exist
while the other is not felt at all.

A prominent instructor in a Southern college
says in a published article that what we call inbred
sin is only a " liability to sin." This, as the reader sees, is the same thought just advanced, only in
different words. Moreover, when this definition
is examined it is nothing after all but saying that
we are free moral agents, for we cannot think of
freedom and the probationary state of man without the accompanying necessary idea of liability to
sin. But certainly liability to sin is one thing, and

a proneness or tendency to do so, which we find
to be the character of inbred sin, is another thing.
So the learned Doctor's explanation cannot be
accepted, and fails because it does not go far
enough and deep enough.

After men have exhausted their ingenuity in
finding proper titles for the dark indwelling something in the regenerated soul, the Lord speaks,
and settles the matter by names and terms that
throw light at once upon the subject and ought to
satisfy the mind.

We have already anticipated some of these
names, and now call attention to a few.

One is the " carnal mind."

About this the Bible speaks in Romans viii. 7,
saying that "the carnal mind is enmity against
God: for it is not subject to the law of God,
neither indeed can be." If this be so, what can
regeneration do with it? If converting grace can
change it, then the Scripture made a mistake in
saying "neither indeed can be." Let the reader
look at the verse again. " The carnal mind . . .
is not subject to the law of God, neither indeed
can be!" These words are the funeral knell to
the Zinzendorfian idea of regeneration. According to this verse the carnal mind cannot be regen-

erated. It is overshadowed and overpowered in regeneration, and *destroyed* in sanctification.

Another scriptural name is the "flesh."

This, as previously stated, does not mean the human body. If so, the Greek word *soma* would have been used. Instead of this word we have the term *sarx*, which Paul almost invariably uses to indicate the fleshly principle or carnal mind. From a failure to recognize this has proceeded the mistake of many in afflicting and punishing the *body* as the seat of sin, when the word "flesh" (*sarx*) as used in the Epistles referred not to the physical man, but to a fleshly principle in the soul; in a word, to carnality.

A third name in the Bible is "body of sin."

The reader will notice the difference between our bodies proper and the members of our body. On the Gulf of Mexico we have a crab one peculiarity of which is that if you pull one of his legs off, and then turn him loose and give him time, he will sprout another leg to take its place; but if you take the crab and crush his *body* with the heel of your shoe, he will sprout no more legs.

So in regard to the "*body* of sin" which is left in us after regeneration. We begin life with this inherited "body of sin." It soon sends forth its

sprouts, limbs, and members. We become convicted over the sprouts and members, for which
alone we feel personally accountable. Repentance
is felt over one's own misdeeds; and the cry of
every penitent who is seeking salvation is: " Lord,
have mercy on me, and forgive *my* sins." The
grace of regeneration washes away personal sins
and guilt. The members of the body of sin instantly drop off; but the " body of sin," the inherited Adamic sin, remains within. The carnal
mind is not subject to the law of God, neither indeed can be. After a little this " body of sin "
begins to sprout forth, or shoot out new members,
in the form of wrong thoughts, tempers, desires,
words, and actions. The man grieves, confesses;
and God forgives again, and away fall off the
members as before. But the " body of sin " being left within, the outcroppings, or offshoots, of
evil continue. Now if the Christian will come to
God asking not for recovering and forgiving
grace, but pleading for the *destructive* power of
sanctification on the body of sin, he will cease to
sprout tempers and conduct that humbled him to
the dust; and he will enter at once upon a life
that is pure, beautiful, joyful, and unutterably
blessed.

A fourth name God gives to inbred sin is the " old man."

This does not mean Satan, for the devil is not a man at all. With the rest of the angels, fallen and unfallen, he is a different order of being. Moreover Satan is never to be destroyed, while the " old man " is to be crucified and destroyed.

The " old man " was born in the garden of Eden about six thousand years ago. He is very properly called the " old man." He is not Adam, but the dark result of something that Adam did under the temptation of the devil. In a word, the reader sees that the expression, "the old man," stands for depravity, or that bias to evil communicated to the human race by the fall of Adam as our federal head.

This " old man " is in every heart that is born into the world. He is in every child. The infant cooing in the arms of its mother, or lying like a little snow blossom on the pillow in its cradle, has this " old man " in its heart. If there could be such a thing as a moral microscope, we could see the hideous features and form of original sin in that infantile soul.

It is not long before the dark inheritance, or indweller, becomes manifest. At the age of six

months and less you will see an infant perfectly
infuriated with its mother or nurse, and going
through actions that, projected in the life of an
adult, would mean murder.   At two years of age
the child will tell a lie, before it knows what a
falsehood is.   It will be cunning before it realizes
what deceit is, and steal when it has not yet com-
prehended the character and sinfulness of theft.

The nature of sin, so far as the human race is
concerned, is older than the act of sin or the
transgression itself.   In the fall of the angels the
sinful act antedated, necessarily, the sinful nature; but with us the nature antedates the act.
This nature, evidencing and announcing itself in
a bias to sin, is called the "old man."

But some one asks: " Is it possible that this
' old man' is left in the heart after regeneration?"

The reply is that such is the statement of the
Bible, and that such is the experience of the soul.

The simple explanation of its remaining is seen in
the fact that when we go to God as repenting sinners, and in the name of Christ, we do not ask
pardon for Adam's sin, but for our own.   We
never think of Adam at such a time; we are
thinking of what we did, and it is this that bows

down the soul. Suppose the penitent had made
such a supplication as: " Lord, forgive me for the
sin of Adam! " To formulate such a prayer and
look at it is to see its absurdity. How can we
ask God to forgive us for another man's sin?
How could God forgive us for another man's sin?
Common sense will answer both questions by saying that both cases are impossible.

The conclusion inevitably reached is that what
cannot be justified or pardoned certainly cannot
be regenerated. And this is the philosophy of a
remaining principle of evil in the soul after regeneration. The Adamic sin transmitted to us cannot be pardoned; and hence remains an unregenerated principle within, whose stirrings, uprisings,
and resistances we feel unmistakably and sadly
enough until the destroying work of sanctification
takes place.

An objection urged against this is that Paul
says in 2 Corinthians v. 17: " If any man be in
Christ, he is a new creature: old things are
passed away; behold, all things are become
new." According to this, says the objector, the
" old man" has become new in regeneration, for
the passage quoted says that " *all things* are become new."

The reply to this is that the Revised Version reads as follows: " Old things are passed away; behold, they are become new." The word " all " is dropped. Besides this, we must all admit that God cannot contradict himself. He never says that the old man becomes the new man, but that the old man is mortified, crucified, destroyed, put off, and after that we put on the new man.

There is one thing that can never become new, and that is the "old man." "The carnal mind is not subject to the law of God, neither indeed can be." Life is not put into the old man, but he is put to death. He does not merge into and become the new man, but is slain, and the new man takes his place in the heart.

A certain confusion has arisen in some minds, from attributing a meaning to regeneration that God never gave to it, and that cannot be found in any Lexicon, English or Greek. Regeneration does not mean "death," but "life." The old man does not need life, he has too much of that already. He needs to die. Regeneration does not bring death, but life; it is the life of God implanted in the soul. Once dead in sins, we are now quickened and live unto God. But life is not death, and here is something in the soul that God says is to die.

There has been a birth, now comes a crucifixion. A new creature has been born into the kingdom; now an old creature is to die right before the eyes of that same rejoicing, shouting, new creature. We being regenerated are permitted to attend the funeral of the "old man." When we see his head drop and feel that he is dead, we return home with shining face and say that we are sanctified.

To sum it all up in a word, the " old man " is not changed, but killed; not converted, but crucified; not saved with the washing of regeneration, but burned out by the baptism of the Holy Ghost and fire. It is not regeneration that settles him, but the blessing of entire sanctification.

CHAPTER XIII.

WE desire to give a likeness of the "old man" that will be remembered. As his features are sketched, the reader may compare the picture with what he finds now, or remembers once to have had in his heart, and be sad or glad accordingly.

He is a cold "old man."

He is opposed to all religious warmth and demonstrativeness. A shout of joy in church or at a camp meeting nearly throws him into a congestive chill. He likes meetings that are frigid and rigid. He believes in frost in the choir, snow in the pew, and an icicle six feet long in the pulpit. A picture of the Ship of Zion surrounded with great spiritual icebergs, hung up in the church library would be according to his taste.

One may start out on the day's duties with a warm heart secured in answer to a fervent morning prayer, but the "old man" will cool off the heart before ten o'clock. The soul may be revived by public worship, greatly exhilarated and

(123)

gladdened by protracted or camp meeting exercises, but the chill of his presence is soon felt
coming on again, and after a few hours or a few
days the soul is back in its former state of coldness and indifference. The " old man " stretched
as it were upon the soul is continually striking
the chill of its freezing presence into the spirit.
A constant spiritual rubbing by prayer and Church
work is needed to keep up anything like spiritual
warmth.

When the " old man " is gone it is both delightful and wonderful to note the undeparting heat
of the soul. The heart feels warm, and remains
warm all the time.

He is an easily offended " old man."

He seems to be looking out for slights. Two
people cannot be seen speaking together but the
" old man " translates it to mean, and persuades
the man to believe, that he is the subject of discus-
sion. There are countless other topics upon
which two people could converse without thinking
of the party in question; but no, the hypersensi-
tive spirit is convinced that present parties are
struck at, and being criticised and ridiculed.
Evidently something about his or her dress, or
something connected with them, is absorbing the

mind and employing the colloquial powers of those two whisperers.

This being the case, at once the backbone begins to stiffen, and the nostrils to inflate. The mental debate going on now is whether or not to be decidedly cool hereafter to those aforesaid innocent parties, who, unconscious of the swelling " old man " in the neighborhood, had been quietly conversing about a child that was sick with the measles.

The presence of the " old man " necessitates the nicest of handling of some people. So many visits a year are absolutely essential to keep on amicable terms. A prompt rushing around to the house in case of sickness in the family must take place, or you must prepare to be socially frozen by a distant bow or an icy smile at the next meeting on street or in parlor.

Great wrongs like the following make life a burden: He was not invited to sit on the platform! He was not allowed to lead the singing, or to conclude with prayer! His name appeared third instead of second or first in some published article or important resolutions! Alas, now! what does it avail to live any longer? Let me die. Behold nothing profits or contents, so long as something or somebody is seen sitting at the king's gate.

When the fires of sanctification burn out the "old man," all this sad experience ends, and Paul's description applies—"Not easily provoked." The man is thinking so little of himself that he hardly knows when he is insulted. We recall an instance, where the President of a large religious body shook his finger violently in a certain direction while uttering severe things about a man who would produce schism in the church. The brother thus assailed, cried out "Amen!" feeling perfectly innocent of the charge; and did not know for months afterwards that he was the man referred to. Not easily provoked.

Get the " old man " out, and any seat will do. Platforms lose their glory, varying treatment fails to disturb. In all things the man has learned to be content. He has shot ahead of Diogenes, who was so far from being contented with his life in a tub that he wanted Alexander to get out of his light. Whereas when we get depravity out of the heart, Alexander can stand where he pleases, we have a blessing in which we live that satisfies us, whether we are in the shade or sunshine.

He is a talkative " old man."

In spite of all caution, watchfulness, and severe self-restraint, suddenly the tongue will begin at a wrong rate and in a wrong spirit. For a half dozen hours we run well, and lo! in the seventh hour the regretted speech is made. We visit several families, determined not to be entrapped into saying anything that is not in perfect harmony with the spirit of love; when lo! at the fourth house a circle of bright people is met, whose tongues are rattling, and before one knows it, the blood gets warm, the thoughts excited, the powers of speech become suddenly animated, the tongue lubricated, and things are said that cost sighs, tears, confessions, and promises of amendment to God. The " old man " seems to take advantage of favoring circumstances to awaken the frivolous, hysterical, or unkind spirit as it may be. Sigh, grieve, promise, as one will, not to do so again—it happens again and again, until God takes out the " old man."

How difficult it is to retain bad news so long as inbred sin is in the heart! The tendency is to confide the painful tidings to wife or friend. The breast is burdened with the secret of a brother's fall. " O how sad! Have you heard about poor Jones? It is shocking." Then follows the history of the fall with a strange inward relish over the imparted information. The sigh is heard —but there is the strange enjoyment in confiding the secret to another. It is only told to two others besides the wife or husband; and each one tells it to two others besides, and so it is not long before the town, State, and country have the news that was "so sad and shocking."

Get the "old man" out, and the power to retain sad and bad information, and to be silent generally, actually becomes like a new gift to the soul. You do not care to whisper around these things. The ear becomes a graveyard for countless things heard, and there is no trumpet of an archangel around to blow them into resurrection form.

The "old man" is a great fault-finder.

We have a certain bird in the South that sails high in the air in graceful circles. Round and round it goes with wonderfully observant eye on the land. Wide forests of fragrant pine toss their branches in the sunlight underneath the dizzy flight, but this circling bird does not care for aromatic pine boughs. It passes over broad meadows and pastures, but it is not on the search for, and cares not for, clover blossoms. With like indifference it refuses to look upon the pink and white blossoms of the orchard. The landscape spreads in rare loveliness far beneath, and unrolls before the flying bird, but he is not after and cares nothing for landscape beauties. He is looking for something that looks black, and lies right still on the ground. By and by he spies it, some say that he smells it. Anyhow he begins to descend rapidly in spiral curves nearer and nearer until at last with hovering wings he alights near by or upon the silent form. It is a carcass! And now he begins to pull and haul on one side, while the rest of his family pull away at the other. Some have beheld the scene. The bird is called a buzzard.

In the regenerated man a strange resemblance in conduct is seen. The "old man" accounts for it. Many times it manifests itself in listening to a sermon. Some people come not to hear the truth, and not to see beauties and excellences in the discourse. A hundred good things are said, but the "old man" is not after good things. It is not fragrant pine branches and clover blossoms he is after. He is looking for something dead and objectionable, something that smacks of error, a grammatical blunder, an unfortunate and unwise speech. In a word, he wants a carcass to light upon. Suddenly he sees it. Next morning at the

9

breakfast table he begins the pulling and hauling
process: " Wife, did you hear what that man said
last night?" Promptly on the other side of the
carcass, taking hold and beginning to pull, she also
replies: "Yes, husband; I heard him say so and
so." Then the children chime in, each one taking hold of some part of the sermon or conversation or occurrence, and jerking and dragging it all
over the breakfast table.

Years afterwards the father and mother of the
family begin to wonder why their children have
no reverence for the pulpit and the Bible. They
stay from church and laugh at religion and all holy
things. The explanation is that they were so in-
structed by example to pull and haul at ministers,
sermons, doctrines, and experiences of the Christian life, that they have grown up argumentative,
fault-finding, and skeptical.

It is wonderful with what a perfect absence of
the critical faculty we listen to indifferent sermons,
or behold blemishes in consecrated lives when the
" old man " is taken out of the heart. The grammatical blunder in the pulpit, the sophomoric style,
the historic misstatement, the inaccurate Scripture
quotation are all overlooked and condoned for as
the eye takes in pleasanter things as seen in the

earnestness and devotion of the person who may be preaching or living before us.

He is a bitter " old man."

Never was there a gland in the body that more certainly secreted saliva, bile, or gall than does the "old man " generate bitterness. As the hours go by there is a steady drip, drip, drip in the heart until it suddenly overflows on some slight provocation, and is emptied on the head of the wife or husband. Instantly repentance sets in, apologies are made to the injured, forgiveness is sought and obtained of God, and life is begun again fair and promising. This time you intend being very careful; the door of the lips is guarded, and all goes well for awhile. Meanwhile the " old man," glandlike, drips on within the heart, and suddenly on returning home from the street, store, or farm, tired and jaded, the provocation comes from an unexpected quarter and over goes the full heart again!—this time on a child or servant, or an animal. Now then for confession, repentance, sighs, and tears again. Again God is entreated, and the same old prayer is offered: " Lord, forgive." And the Lord does forgive. He does what we ask him. The suppliant, we notice, does not ask to be sanctified, and that the " old man " should be put to death and cast out. No, he does not believe in sanctification. He believes in pardon and growth in grace. So on he goes, and as he grows the "old man" grows also. And the drip, drip, drip of bitterness goes on inside, and the sudden overflowings of gall as described are periodic as the tides.

The writer recalls a sermon he once preached before his sanctification at a large camp ground. The Spirit fell on the word, and salvation flowed. A prominent minister, meeting the writer after the signal victory, called him "a prince of Israel." How this did please the "old man" that dwelt inside! At once a plume of gratified vanity was hoisted, and the invisible feathers waved in the wind of human praise. At the same time came a sudden inclination to return home. Better leave now with a fine camp meeting reputation than stay and risk it with another sermon, that may not measure up to the other. Done! Go we must, in spite of urgings to remain. Important duties call home. Heavy pastoral work must be met. So we covered up the voice within, and go we did with the glow of victory in the heart and the aforesaid feathers waving in the wind. A prince of Israel so acknowledged and called was going home. He will tell his wife what a sermon he preached; what an altar scene followed; how a prominent minister said he was ''a prince.'' The wife must be informed what a husband she has. So the prince and his plume returned home. Meantime the '' old man'' is not dead. The drip, drip is going on, unnoticed in the princely heart; and suddenly, just eight hours after the signal victory on the camp ground, the prince with his feathers, after having told his wife, like Haman told his, what a wonderful man he was, this same prince with his feathers under a slight provocation got mad in the midst of his family! Off went the feathers and down went the prince.

When God casts the '' old man '' out, and the New Man takes his place, how marvelous and blessed the change! Instead of these secretions of gall there is a constant dripping of sweetness within as if a lump of golden honey was lodged somewhere in the heart. Let the reader obtain the experience and know for himself.

He is a gloomy '' old man.''

Sudden spells of melancholy, or fits of blues, constitute one of the features of the regenerated life. Regeneration does not produce it, but it comes in spite of regeneration. To many Christians it is unaccountable. One day they are bright and cheerful, and the next day this peculiar gloom settles upon the soul. Sometimes one awakens with this heavy something on the heart and weighing down the spirits. There is a disinclination to talk—worse still, a disposition to be fault-finding and snappish. The person does not know what brought it on, but on awakening in the morning found the incubus on the heart.

This is the day, if the spell is on the husband, that the wife asks no questions. With a swift glance over the breakfast table she sees that something is wrong, and is careful to say nothing, or if anything at all, speaks in the most soothing manner. Think of a wife studying her husband's face to see if she can break to him a piece of news, or ask a question. It is a peculiar day in the family history. The children are shy of " Papa " on such days. The meals are eaten in silence. The man gulps down his food with his eyes on his plate, and communicates only in monosyllables and grunts. He despises himself for the churlishness that is in him, but feels utterly powerless to shake it off. Poor fellow! he does not know what it is, and does not dream that Christ can take it out forever.

Sometimes it is the wife upon whom the " spell "

comes. This is the day on which the husband takes lunch down town; this is the day that the peculiar music of hand-slapping upon the cheeks of the children reverberates through the house. Whippings and scoldings abound that day. Nothing seems to go right. The steam of inbred sin works itself off in voice-raisings and hand motions of punitive character.

The writer knew a lady who on a slight provocation on one of these gloomy days struck at one of the children with a switch. From the careless and vehement motion of the rod, another child was struck accidentally, who promptly blubbered, when immediately the lady whipped the blubberer, and in the commotion that followed never stopped until she whipped the whole family. After that, with fearful convictions of what she had done, she took her Bible and went to the woods, where she spent three hours in bitter reflection, repentance, and prayer, and came back with an "Amazing grace! how sweet the sound!" look on her face. She was forgiven, it was true, but what a picture lesson to her family!

The writer has known ladies to go off to themselves on one of these gloomy days of the "old man" administration, and cry out their heaviness

and blueness, not dreaming that inbred sin was
the cause of the whole trouble. They thought it
was forebodings of ill, or memory of past sorrows,
etc., but the real cause they did not know, and so
wept themselves into temporary relief, only to cry
again in like manner in a few days or weeks.

The world's explanation of this moody condition
is that the wind is in the east, when really it is the
" old man" in the heart.

The world says, again, that we have gotten out of
the wrong side of the bed; when the fact is, if we
get inbred sin out of us, it does not matter which
side of the bed we get out at, whether on the right
or left, whether over the head or foot, or even if
we break through the slats and come from under
the bed—still we will always come out right.

A lady told the author that her father would be
like a beam of sunshine one day, and lo! the next
morning he would appear grum, glum, and dumb.
He looked as if he had heard that half the town
was dead, and the other half was dying, and the
hearse was on its way for himself. In this mourn-
ful frame he would address himself to the task of
carving the meat at breakfast and in the most lu-
gubrious tone say, " Daughter, will you have a
piece of the beefsteak?" and she, bright, cheery,

winning, would say, "Yes, father, but there is no use of being so broken-hearted about it!"

Here was a man who had been the center of an admiring social circle the evening before. His wit had flashed. His wonderful memory and gifted tongue had charmed the roomful of guests, his laughter had rung out cheerily and contagiously—when lo! presto, change! Next morning there is left for the enjoyment of the family itself a man of groans and sighs and monosyllables and depressed appearance generally. The lines of his face that were all turned up the night before are now all turned down. He seems to be sitting under a willow, a statue of a weeping Niobe is close by, the sun is set, darkness has settled upon the plain, and a gray mist has crept in from the sea. A cemetery glistens faintly under the cold starlight—and what is the use of living anyhow? All this is wrought out by the presence of the "old man" in the heart.

When inbred sin is taken out, the awakening in the morning is one of peace and gladness. The whole day becomes like a sweet bright leaf turned by the hand of God. The world soon takes notice of a man who is even-tempered and sweet-spirited at every meal, in every hour, and under every circumstance. This is the kind of Christian living the world craves to see, and this is the char- acter of life that a genuine sanctification will pro- duce.

He is a man-fearing " old man."

It is marvelous how he stands in awe of men, especially of men in high place and authority. Their voices and footfalls seem to send a thrill of terror through him.

Akin to this is his disposition to conform to the world. He, while doing this, would have you call it prudence, tact, or policy; but it is really con- formity.

He believes in churches, but wants them run to please people of the world. Nothing must be done that will provoke the world's criticism or displeasure.

Think of it! a church managed so as to please a God-forgetting, Christ-crucifying world. If there were such a church, God would spew it out of his mouth!

He is a tyrannical " old man."

On the shoulders of Sindbad dropped an old man of the sea, who made him go wherever he de- sired. The afflicted man resorted to various ex- pedients to get rid of him, but for a great while to no purpose; the old creature of the sea clung to him and ruled his motions as he brooded, a dead, dark weight upon his back.

Not less tyrannical is the "old man" that we are speaking of in this volume. Many a time the child of God desires to do certain things, discharge certain duties, and yet realizes at the same time something powerful within opposing and pulling back.

The voice of the Spirit bids one go to a neighbor and clear up some trouble or misunderstanding; the Christian obediently starts, comes in sight of the house, and at once the "old man" arrests his progress, sends him off another way, and finally he returns home without having done the Heaven-impressed duty.

Again the Spirit urges one to come to the altar; but the "old man" keeps him rooted to his seat, and, with a leadenlike sensation in heart, mind, and members, the man feels unable to move.

Still again the Christian would confess a wrong to some one, and instantly the "old man" paralyzes the tongue in the presence of the wronged party.

He is a corrupt "old man."

God himself says so in Ephesians iv. 22: "That ye put off . . . the old man, which is

corrupt." It is the presence of inbred sin in the
heart that accounts for desires and imaginations
that are not chaste. It is wonderful how pure the
thoughts, and even the dreams, become when
God's holy fire falls upon the " old man."

He is a deceitful " old man."

A person will think he is dead a hundred times,
when he is only slumbering and resting. Like a
certain animal in our Southern forests, he can
play the opossum. He can counterfeit death.
He often lies low during a Holiness revival. He
is afraid of the baptism of fire falling upon the
human soul. He has need to be afraid.

After a rough handling from the pulpit, or upon
hearing a vigorous prayer, or melted by some
discourse or touching hymn, or chastened by
some heavy sorrow, the "old man " will make out
that he is converted, and even that he is dead.

The writer thought that he was dead many
times before the Lord slew him. More than once
he carried him to the cemetery and buried him;
and lo! the "old man" would arise from the grave,
take a near cut to town, and open the door for us
on our arrival, saying with a smile: " I beat you
back, you see." We have been driving him in a
hearse to the burial ground, when he would get

out of the coffin, take a seat by the driver, and assist in the rest of the expedition, which it is needless to say would be cut short.

Christians under certain preaching or religious singing have had hearty bits of weeping over their sins and unworthiness; after which the "old man" would be quiet for weeks, and they would think that he was drowned. But it is not in the power of water to destroy him; it is the blood of Christ alone which cleanseth from all sin.

That sermon, no matter how powerful, was never preached that can destroy the "old man." Equally helpless are hymn and prayer. It takes the divine hand and power to hurl him from the heart, and rid the soul of his dark and grewsome presence forever. Hence for this purpose was the Son of God manifested, that he might destroy this work of the devil.

CHAPTER XIV.

IT is a great pity that men will not allow God to do his work in his own way. One of the results of the fall is seen in perverted moral perceptions and judgment. Men do not believe in nor take to God's ways. The wisdom of the world is set against and over the wisdom of God. Every sinner starts out at some time to save himself. Instead of coming to Christ, he tries reformation, morality, benevolence, churchgoing and every other expedient to be saved outside of Christ. It is only when he has failed in them all that he gives up in self-despair, looks to Christ, and receives salvation.

In like manner Christians err in seeking for sanctification or holiness of heart and life. They look in every direction and try every way before coming to Christ, who is "made unto us sanctification" as well as pardon or justification.

Surely every Christian desires to be rid of the presence of the "old man." Who would want to retain him in the heart? That people do not is seen in the universal hope of finally getting rid of

(142)

him, and beheld in the various efforts put forth to secure this deliverance.

It is curious to notice that the flight of the centuries has not brought wisdom to the great mass of the church, and that countless thousands are floundering to-day where people struggled hopelessly in the Dark Ages.

It is amazing to see how persistent the human heart is to look away from acts of sovereign grace and try to build up a righteousness of their own. The old desire to save or purify self is not yet eliminated, we see, in regeneration. The *full* work and power of Christ is not yet apprehended save in word only. The lip declares him a perfect Saviour, but the heart has not yet so apprehended him.

This was in Paul's mind when he asked the Galatians who had bewitched them: "Having begun in the Spirit, are ye now made perfect by the flesh?"

At another time he laments that Israel is blinded in part—going about to establish their own righteousness, and not obtaining the righteousness which is by faith.

The Galatian mistake and the blunder of Israel have been perpetuated from age to age. The old folly was seen all through the Dark Ages in the endeavor of men to obtain holiness, and is just as apparent to-day. Let us glance and see how men have tried and are trying, to get rid of the " old man."

One method is seclusion. Men and women retired to monasteries and convents, to dens and caves of the earth, to find deliverance from sin. They thought they could mope the " old man " to death; that he would gradually expire through the effect of isolation.

But history tells us that the Church was never more corrupt than when it went into retirement. Christ went among men. Purity is never to be more stalwart than when it moves among the walks, haunts, and market places of men. It is in the world, but not of the world.

On the other hand, the " old man " is wonderfully vigorous in lonely hours and sequestered spots. So says experience and history.

Another method is flagellation.

Whips were plaited and faithfully applied to the body. The crack of the scourge resounded in lonely cloisters. Every species of physical torture was resorted to, to compel the lurking principle of evil to vacate the heart.

And yet the " old man " remained undisturbed within. The cut of the lash never troubled him. There never was a whip made, or cracker plaited, no matter how long or keen, that could reach the " old man." The flesh might be riven by the cruel scourge into ghastly seams, and the very bones exposed, but no thong of leather ever touched him. It does not, so to speak, come in miles of him; for the " old man " is not in the bone, blood, and muscle at all, but resides in the soul. Hence the crack of the whip is so much music to him. He smiles at the stupidity that tries to remedy a spiritual condition with a material weapon.

Men have smiled at this folly of the Dark Ages; and yet the same mistake is repeated in what is called evangelical times, and by Protestant people. What is the beating of the breast, and calling one's self by harsh and bitter terms, but a kindred mistake.

A third method is fasting.

For centuries men tried to starve out this principle or body of sin. They became emaciated and looked like skeletons, while the " old man " remained as fresh and vigorous within as ever.

Has the regenerated man not noticed on his fast days that his sinful nature was unusually lively and vigorous; that the tendency to irritabil-

10

ity and petulance was increased with the weakening body?

The fact is that the " old man " does not live on bread and meat, but subsists on controversy. Hence as we grow weak with protracted fasts, in the endeavor to achieve heart purity, we discover that we make no headway. Our most mortifying falls have occurred on our fast days.

A fourth method is a looking to time for deliverance.

The flight of years is trusted to eradicate the evil propensity. Men comfort themselves with the thought that somehow, in some way, the years as they pass will soak up or fly away with the inward evil.

This of course is exalting time to the plane and place of a Saviour and purifier, and credits it with a divine work. And of course also there is bound to be lamentable failure. There is nothing in time to purify the soul. The mere flight of years can have no transforming effect on the heart. The " old man " has nothing to fear from time, for he is already six thousand years old. He will outlive any man or woman who is three score and ten, and will outlive many generations to come. What does he care for time?

A fifth method or hope is seen in a certain dependence on, or expectation from, old age.

The idea of some is that gray hairs will settle their many evil propensities and troubles. Parents say about their children: "O, they will come out all right when they get older." Old age is their Saviour. Accumulating years, with their gathering infirmities, diseases, wrinkled face, and snowy hair, is to be the deliverer.

The "old man" is made to laugh again at the additional folly. He knows that the flight of years only fastens his grip on the soul; and that all the change that takes place in the case is that he shifts his perch from one resting place to another as the years increase, and flaps his sable wings on another roost in the same soul. For instance, he springs from the appetites of the young man to the love of money in the old man.

It is time to quit deifying gray hairs. They are all right and a crown of glory when found in the way of righteousness, but a fool's cap to one who lives in sin. They look venerable, but we little know what that same gray-haired man is thinking about. If we did, we might start with surprise.

A sixth method is seen in the growth theory.

This is the heresy in many churches to-day,

that purity comes by growth in grace. This
teaching, it is seen at a glance, uncrowns Christ,
robs him of his peculiar glory of sanctifying the
Church as mentioned in Ephesians, and transforms what is recognized in the Bible as a divine
work into a mere evolution or development.

As remarked in a previous chapter, to prove the
growth theory of purity there should be analogies
in nature for the figure, plain statements of the
Word of God, and the confirmation of human testimony. It is hardly necessary to say that such
proof has not been, and never will be, found.

It is true that the Bible says, " Grow in
grace; " but let the reader mark that it says " *in*
grace." It does not say grow up to or into grace.
We are told to " *go on to* perfection; " but in another connection altogether we are commanded
to " grow *in* grace "—*i. e*, grow *in* the grace *into
which ye have been inducted by divine power*.

Much dependence is placed on the saying of
Christ about " first the blade, then the ear, then
the full corn in the ear; " but if this proves
growth into sanctification, it also declares the fact
of growth into regeneration, which the Church will
hardly allow. If the critics insist that the " full
corn " stands for sanctification, and that it was

reached by growth, then the "blade" or the "ear" was also reached by growth. As the logicians say, this proves too much, and so proves nothing.

The fact is, according to an author in New England, the blade, ear, and full corn in the ear represent epochs and not processes. The three stand for pardon, purity, and maturity.

Another misunderstood passage, and that has been quoted to prove the growth theory of holiness, is found in Ephesians iv. 11–15: "And he gave some, apostles; and some, prophets; and some, evangelists; and some, pastors and teachers: for the perfecting of the saints, for the work of the ministry, for the edifying of the body of Christ: till we all *come* in the unity of the faith, and of the knowledge of the Son of God, *unto a perfect man*, unto the measure of the stature of the fullness of Christ. That we henceforth be no more children, tossed to and fro, and carried about with every wind of doctrine, by the sleight of men, and cunning craftiness, whereby they lie in wait to deceive. But speaking the truth in love, may *grow up* into him in all things, which is the head, even Christ."

The reader is requested to observe the Italicized

words in the passage just quoted. We have done so to show more clearly that the growth referred to here takes place *after* we have obtained the blessing of perfection or fullness of Christ. Paul does not say that we "*grow* " into a perfect man, but that we " *come* " unto a perfect man; and, *after that*, " speaking the truth in love we *grow* up into him in all things."

It is painful to see the thousands in Christ's Church switched off on this side track, and while there is a great ringing of bells and puffing of engines, the fact is apparent to all that they are not getting anywhere—that the desired destination of Purity or Perfect Love is not being reached—in a word, they are side tracked!

Changing the figure, God's people are growing the plants of the Christian graces abundantly, a beautiful arbor is formed out of them, but in the face of their luxuriance, again and again the " old man " parts the spiritual and Church shrubbery, and, looking out, says: " I am in here just the same."

A momentary consternation is felt by the Christian after one of these inbred sin manifestations, and he or she jumps to the conclusion at once: " I must take up more Church work—join a few more societies—multiply my Christian activities, and the " old man " will finally be strangled and choked within me by the very superabundance of blossoms, leaves, flowers, and fruit of the Christian life."

At this the " old man " smiles in the heart, and quietly watches his victim planting new shrubs, broadening and heightening the Christian graces, and so forth. When just as a sigh of relief is felt by the growing brother, the " old man " shakes the religious timber and underbrush and says: " I am in here, and you must not forget it."

From stewards' meeting, trustees' meeting, Quarterly Conference, and District Conference; from Conventions, Missionary Societies, Ladies' Aid Societies, and all such things, the brother or sister returns home and suddenly the "old man" stands revealed in hot words, hasty acts, resounding slaps, ill-natured speech before the gaze of astonished servants and frightened children.

O that common sense would come to the help of the people here! Let us recall how a handkerchief is made white and clean. Do we sew new, clean linen around the edges, and so grow it pure? Do we take two other handkerchiefs and put the dirty handkerchief between the two, and say: " Here is

purity?'' We all know better. We take the soiled
linen and plunging it into soap and water that has
fire under it, lo! the handkerchief is washed white.

So God says that with refiner's fire and fuller's
soap he will purify the sons of Levi, his own servants.

How does the mother cleanse the face of her
child? Does she look at the dirty countenance of
her boy, and say: '' My son, I see that you are not
clean, but I am trusting that in the flight of years
and through various processes and evolutions of
your physical nature your face will finally develop
or grow into cleanness.'' No, indeed; no mother
talks such nonsense; but instead she takes her
earth-soiled boy by the back of the neck with one
hand, and with the other souses a sponge of soap
and warm water over his face, and lo! the child is
clean. The boy was her son before; the mother
did not disown him on account of the stained and
spotted face. The washing she gave him was not
to make the lad her child, but to make him her
clean child.

Sanctification, or the destruction of the '' old
man '' in the heart, does not make us sons and
daughters of the Almighty; that we were before, but
it transforms us into his clean and pure children.

CHAPTER XV.

A SEVENTH human method of dealing with the "old man" is found in the repression theory.

This teaching abounds in England to-day. The erroneous doctrine is seen permeating the books of her most spiritual writers. The "old man" is recognized as remaining in the heart after regeneration. They affirm that he cannot be destroyed, but is held in a state of subjection and suppression.

The trouble about this method or theory is that it is calculated to fill the Christian heart and life with a vague dread of the sudden uprising of the "old man." When men sailed across the seas in slave ships filled with human beings in captivity there was bound to be an uneasy feeling day and night, that there would be a sudden rush for liberty, a bursting open of the hatchway and a dreaded and dreadful appearing on the deck. In like manner there is a secret uneasiness in the soul in regard to sudden ebullitions and manifestations of

(153)

suppressed dispositions and tendencies in the open life. Such a state is not reconcilable with the thought of perfect rest.

Again, the suppression of the " old man" means the nondoing of much that should be done in the Christian life.

Suppose a man is struggling for his life with a foe, finally overthrows him and gets him down; yet he dares not leave the prostrate adversary, knowing that the instant he does the fallen man will arise and grapple with him again. One is practically as helpless and useless at the time as the other.

In like manner the Christian, according to the repression theory has the " old man " down; but as inbred sin is not dead, but simply repressed, the Christian's whole power and attention is needed to keep the suppressed evil down continually. The Church is calling for him to enter on various religious activities, but he looks up and says: " I would like to help you, but I cannot do it; for I have all that I can attend to right here in keeping the " old man" down.

This is evidently the case with many thousands. People are kept busy in taking care of and controlling themselves. If they relax this diligent, unceasing, inward repressing power a moment, behold, the " old man " is on his feet, and the conflict begins again.

It is wonderful how long inbred sin will remain in a suppressed condition, and then suddenly come forth from its hiding and resting place.

The writer once knew a local preacher who becoming angered over a sermon on full salvation preached by his pastor, called out from the congregation in a sharp, excited way, and accused the preacher of the hour of injuring the church by such preaching. The interrupter evidently thought he had the audience on his side. The pastor thus interrupted replied that he would leave it to the audience to say whether he had not preached the truth and in the spirit of the Master; and so asking all to stand on their feet who thus indorsed him, the entire audience with half a dozen exceptions sprang to their feet. The Spirit of God at the same time fell upon a number, there was shouting and clapping of hands, in the midst of which the pastor invited the people to the altar, when there was a rush. In the morning a note came from the local preacher requesting his church certificate or letter. The pastor at once called on him to dissuade him from his intention. The matter was left for decision with the wife of the local preacher. With the tears falling upon her cheeks she in the course of the conversation said that she would not have had the circumstance of the night before to have happened for a million dollars, and that her husband *had not acted that way before for five years!* The point we make is seen in the Italicized sentence; that the " old man " had slumbered in this local preacher's heart for five years, and then suddenly leaped forth, refreshed from his long rest and disposed to make up for lost time.

An additional trouble with the suppression theory is that it discounts the work of Christ and plainly contradicts the Bible. The Scripture in no place says that the "old man" or inbred sin is to be " kept under " or in a state of subjugation. Paul says, "I keep my body (*soma*) under;" but the flesh (*sarx*) which is the carnal mind or " old man," he says is " crucified " and "*destroyed!*" Truly this last single word of Scripture " destroyed " overturns the reasoning of the Suppressionists.

An eighth human method is what may be called the whitewashing way.

It is strange that things done in the political world should be adopted in the spiritual life. The whitewashing business is as common a spectacle in one as the other. Yet we cannot but remember that an old fence whitewashed is still an old fence.

There is not much seeming difference in the words "whitewashed" and "washed white," and yet all the difference in the character world exists between the two. The first is man's work; the second is God's. The first is skin deep and superficial, the second is soul deep and goes through and through the entire man. The result of one work is a Pharisee, the product of the other is a redeemed and sanctified child of God.

A ninth human mode of obtaining the destruction of sin, or purity, is reformation.

Reformation consists in dropping off some things and taking on some things. Anything rather than God's plan. Rather than let Christ remove the "old man" and clothe us with the New Man, men prefer to keep busy dropping questionable things and taking up better things. But putting silk and broadcloth on a leper never cured the disease, and cutting off his members one by one cannot arrest the malady.

We read once of an hotel keeper who painted over the old sign of a black dragon the more peaceable picture of a lamb. The sign creaked and swung in the wind for years; the rain and snow beat upon it, the storms swept against it season after season. Suddenly one morning after a windy, rainy night the people looked up and saw that the picture of the lamb was washed away, and there was the old black dragon pawing and clawing the air as of yore.

The point and moral of this is that the deeper nature will finally make itself seen. We may put on the appearance of the dove and lamb; we may abound in smiles, voice-cooing, and hand-shaking; but suddenly on some unexpected provocation or assault the " old man " will appear, to our intense mortification and to the astonishment and amusement of our friends.

A preacher recently said to us that he preached to his people the necessity of putting off the " old man" each day, and putting on the New Man; that every day we must get rid of the old dark nature, and that it was an endless work. We replied that we did not have to sandwich our souls that way with the old and the new; a portion of the New Man on top of a remaining portion of the " old man," and then another slice off of the " old man," and then another addition of the New Man. Here again is evident the man salvation idea;

anything rather than let God do the work, now, at once, and forever.

God does not care to have us in such prolonged agony. Such a presentation of holiness utterly destroys the teaching of the Bible in regard to a full and perfect soul rest. How could there be such with this internal convulsion going on all the time?

We told the brother that his presentation of the case reminded us of a monkey story we once heard related by Bishop Kavanaugh. A gentleman, he said, owned one of these frisky animals. It became sick, and a neighbor advised him to have its tail cut off, and the afflicted pet would get well. Calling his cook, the owner told him to take the monkey into the cellar and remove his tail. In a few moments the gentleman heard his monkey give a fearful squeal. There was a stillness of a minute, and then came another shrill cry from the monkey. In a little while a third squeal came up from the cellar, then a fourth rent the air; whereupon the gentleman went down to investigate matters, and found that the cook was cutting off the monkey's tail by inches. His explanation was that he thought it would hurt less to take it off by sections than to cut it all off at one stroke.

This perennial dying, and this protracted agony
and squealing experience is to be seen in the lives
of thousands of good people to-day. They do not
seem to realize that God has power to end all this
at a stroke, of sin elimination, and so cut the work
short in righteousness. The evil is so deep, they
think, and so fixed and so great that it has to be
dealt with by sections, and the deliverance one of
a piecemeal character. They forget what an almighty Saviour we have.

A tenth human plan is seen in the line of edu-
cation and refinement.

The idea of some is that, while the " old man "
cannot be removed, he can be greatly improved,
and so much will he be polished and corrected
that he will not be altogether an unpleasant com-
panion. Hence a general culture is sought after,
from painting China and hammering brass up or
down as pleases the reader. Accomplishments
and trainings of mind and body are suddenly discovered to have moral effect. French, German,
and classic music are to be diligently sought after
for their character transforming power. Even the
drill master and the dancing master are felt to be
contributors to this great character sum.

The result of all this is that the " old man "

simply becomes a polished "old man," and speaks French and German, sings and plays classic music, and is thoroughly at ease in a drawing-room. To the mind of the thinker this metamorphosis makes him all the more dangerous and to be dreaded. The accomplished, polished villain with his set smile and oily manner is more to be feared than the rough boor with a cudgel in his hands. Any one can make the application.

The eleventh hope is located in the deathbed.

Countless thousands of Christians are to-day looking for the hour of dissolution to deliver them from the "old man." Something is to be done by death to relieve them from this awful spiritual incubus.

What strange perversity is that in human nature that makes it turn anywhere and everywhere to escape the acknowledgment and work of a divine Saviour and Sanctifier. Rather than look for holiness as a work wrought by the High and Holy One, men will look to a sepulcher and to a nonentity like death.

This notion is based on the teachings of an old-time heresy which located sin in matter, and hence in the human body. According to this false idea the only hope of a man is to die to escape the sin-

11

ful material enswathement which is called the body.

Any chemist could convince the veriest skeptic in this regard, in a few minutes, that there is no sin in the body, by showing all the component parts, and ocularly proving that we physically are made up entirely of a few chemicals and drugs like soda, lime, iron, etc., that have no moral quality in themselves, much less sin.

Sin is recognized by all spiritually intelligent people to be in the soul. The body does not know what sin is, and is simply a vehicle or instrument of the soul; so that when a man sins it is simply the soul sinning through the body; the soul is using the body as a servant to carry out its designs and desires. Death is but a falling away of the body from around the soul, like scaffolding is taken from a house. The spirit flies away as the body falls into ruins, and takes away with it in its long flight into eternity all that was in it when surprised by death. Hence if sin is left in the soul at death it will be there forever. As the tree falleth, so shall it lie.

The twelfth dream in regard to heart purity arises from the fires of purgatory.

According to this human imagination God is

powerless to take out of the soul in this life the
evil bias or principle planted there by the devil,
and has prepared a place of material fire in which
the soul that has left the body and earth with this
indwelling evil is to be plunged, burned, and purified. But even then the fires burn slowly and
with difficulty, and so much giving and praying is
needed on earth to expedite matters and complete
the work.

We still see how the divine personal work is
banished. Anything rather than have God to purify or sanctify the soul.

Alas for us! if we do not get the " old man " out
before we enter eternity, he will never be taken
out. This indwelling, resident " old man " will
form a peculiar individual type of lost spiritual
life. The Bible recognizes devils in orders of li-
ons, dragons, serpents, etc. So the lost souls of
men will be as clearly and awfully marked and
individualized according to the peculiar development of the " old man " in the soul and life. So in
the character world of the lost will be seen the
fox, wolf, bear, snake, hog, and goat, as adum-
brated in the life on earth, and crystallized forever
in perverted character and undone souls. Made
to be as gods, yet succumbing to the " old man " or

sin principle within, refusing the regenerating grace of God that subdues him, and rejecting the sanctifying grace that expels him, immortal souls under his full weight and influence fall forever from the spiritual and celestial unto planes of beast and devil.

But what if a regenerated man dies with the " old man " still in his soul?

In reply we would say that if a man is really regenerated, when he comes to die, Christ—not death—Christ takes out the " old man," and gives sanctifying grace to the soul. We must remember that sanctification is in the atonement. Jesus Christ is "made unto us wisdom, righteousness, sanctification, and redemption." When we take Christ at the moment of pardon or justification for our Saviour, he becomes to us all that we need, and each one of these great mercies mentioned above will be paid down to the soul in their regular and certain order. Sanctification is in the atonement, as is redemption or the resurrection. Some Christians, from lack of instruction, fail to obtain sanctification until about to die. At that time, on laying everything on the altar—family, friends, property, soul, body, and everything—Jesus Christ, the sanctifying High

Priest of the soul, appears, even though it is at the eleventh hour and the night has come; the fire falls, and the work is wrought in the soul clearly to the beholder. This wonderful lifting up of the soul at the hour or day of dissolution has been called " dying grace;" but there is no such expression in the Bible, and no such separate and distinct blessing. What we call " dying grace " is nothing in the world but sanctification, which many of God's children receive at the eleventh hour, when they could have had it at the second hour; and at death, when it was obtainable in early life.

It is very much like a man who has a large deposit of money in bank; he needs it all day; and just a few minutes before three o'clock, when the bank doors close, he steps up, calls for it, and has it paid down to him. But he could have had it early in the day if he had only asked for it. So this great blessing of the destruction of inbred sin, or the sanctifying of the soul, is in Christ for us. It can be had any moment after regeneration. Alas that so few seek it, that so few get "all on the altar" until the death hour, that so few get the transcendent grace of purity and perfect love until a little while before seeing God!

for the Scripture is perfectly clear here: " Without holiness no man shall see the Lord." The Revised Version says: "Without the sanctification no man shall see the Lord." Christ also speaks, saying: " Blessed are the pure in heart: for they shall see God."

Where God's people have not been informed of this privilege, we see how the grace comes for the first time at death, not by death, as many of us have seen in dying friends and relatives. But if we, as God's people, have been taught concerning the " old man," and our privilege and duty of having him destroyed, and yet through prejudice, spiritual pride, and other reasons refuse to make the consecration and exercise the faith and seek through prayer the blessing that brings the deliverance, then indeed is it questionable whether it will ever be taken out, and we see God. Hence the ground for the words that we uttered some pages back, that if the " old man " is not taken out before we die, he never will be taken out. He is in us forever.

It is to be remembered that no man is condemned for having inbred sin in him, but for keeping it when there is deliverance. Suppose that a person should leave his home some morning unconscious that a keg of powder was underneath his fireplace, and that the fire was rapidly approaching it. He is not long absent before the explosion takes place, and his entire family are killed. Not a soul in the community condemns him, because he was ignorant of the keg of powder and its proximity to the fire. But suppose that upon leaving his house that morning he had seen the keg of powder, its nearness to the fire, and the coals dropping near the keg. Then when the explosion took place, and his family were destroyed, every one would condemn him; for he knew the peril, and had opportunity to remove the cause of danger.

A regenerated man can live for years without condemnation with inbred sin in him, if he does not understand it, nor know the way of deliverance. But when the truth has been preached and light has come, and the gracious deliverance is shown in the blessing of entire sanctification, and the man turns from it all, then condemnation is certain to come, and the question may well arise in the mind whether such a man will ever get inbred sin out, and whether he will ever see God.

The rejection of the Son of God two thousand years ago was the sin of the Jews; and the rejection of the light and work of the Holy Ghost is the sin to-day of some who are called Christians. As a judgment of darkness fell upon the Jews for the first offense, so has the writer seen a similar judgment fall upon Christians for the second. When such a judgment comes upon the spirit, it is no more difficult for a Jew to believe in regeneration through faith in Christ than it is for a Gentile to look for sanctification through the blood of the same divine Saviour.

CHAPTER XVI.

THE DIVINE METHOD OF DEALING WITH THE "OLD MAN."

GOD has a way of proceeding against inbred sin. One may be certain that it is a thorough way, and eminently satisfactory both to the soul and to God.

That way or method has already again and again been anticipated in the foregoing chapters. It is one of extirpation and destruction.

This we would naturally expect from God. Who could believe that he would be satisfied with inbred sin, or the work of the devil left in the heart?

The writer once heard a preacher say that "any experience that was not satisfactory to a Christian could not possibly be so to God." This was a wonderful utterance, and as true as the gospel, for the Word of God teaches the same thing.

The question arises: Can God remove or destroy inbred sin in the soul? If we say that he cannot, then has the devil done a work that God cannot undo, and we have a creature towering above the Creator. In a word, God is not all-powerful. If we say that God can destroy inbred sin but will not, then we have a being in the skies lacking in love and pity for his creatures, and actually allowing sin to abide in the soul when it is in his power to remove it.

The divine command in the Bible is not to "cover sin," but this idea just advanced makes God a coverer of sin as well as man. So we are driven back upon the blessed truth that God can and will destroy all sin in the soul. And this is just what the Bible teaches throughout.

The figures used to describe the work are most powerful.

In one place the symbol of fire is used. There is no more destructive agency than fire. This is recognized in the physical world. God takes this well-known figure of destructive power, and promises the baptism of the Holy Ghost and of fire to burn out the remainder of iniquity.

It was the *fire* laid upon Isaiah's lips that flew like electricity through his being and purged him of iniquity. There was no reference to pardon. The word "purge" refers to the action of fire.

Malachi is clear about it, as he prophesies that the Messiah is going to purify the sons of Levi (not sinners) and purge them with fuller's soap and fire.

John the Baptist talked about it to forgiven people, for according to Luke i. 77 John gave " knowledge of salvation unto his people by the remission of their sins." To these same people who had received remission of sins he promises that Christ would baptize them with the Holy Ghost and with *fire*.

This was first fulfilled on the day of Pentecost, when the "*fire*" fell upon the one hundred and twenty. Peter, in speaking of it afterwards, said that their hearts that day were " purified." Evidently something was destroyed in the souls of the disciples, for they were transformed men ever after. The change that took place was so remarkable that a child in reading the Book of Acts can see it.

This baptism of fire, destructive of sin in that it " purifies the heart " and delivers from man-fear as seen in the case of the disciples, is said by Peter to be for all. He calls it " the promise," as Jesus himself so termed it when he said, " Wait for the promise of the Father." Hence Peter addressing the wondering throng on the morning of Pentecost, said: " The promise is unto you, and to your children, and to all that are afar off, even as many as the Lord our God shall call."

Let the reader remember that a birth is one

thing and a baptism another. Moreover, a baptism follows a birth in the natural world, and does the same in the spiritual life. Have we been born again? Then should we seek at once the baptism of fire that destroys sin and purifies the heart.

A second figure of destruction is that of crucifixion.

There is not a more fearful and certain mode of death known on earth than that of the cross. The crucified man is bound to die. This figure God uses to describe the death of the "old man." Moreover, it is put in a way to show that it is not a gradual lifelong dying, but something accomplished here, hence Paul says: "Knowing this, that our old man is crucified with him, that the body of sin might be destroyed." He brings his own crucifixion forward in a tense that settles the fact that it is done, in the words "I *am* crucified," even as we say to-day, "I *am* sanctified."

We cannot get the idea of regeneration in crucifixion. Just as in the natural life we must be born first before crucifixion is possible, so in the spiritual world birth must come first, and then crucifixion. The life that follows is a most blessed one with Christ living continually in us. As Paul expresses it, "I am crucified with Christ; nevertheless I live; yet not I, but Christ liveth in me."

A third figure is that of utter removal, shown in the words "put off."

Some would read it as if the "old man" was to be put down and kept down; but God says, "put *off*." When a garment is put off, it is certainly not on one nor in one.

A quibble may be made by stating that the command "Put off the old man" is to the Church, and so is a human work or performance after all. But when the quibbler remembers that the Bible also says, "Save yourselves," and yet salvation is of God, the objection falls to the ground.

John the Baptist saw this removal of sin from the soul and declared it in the words, "Behold the Lamb of God that taketh away the sin of the world." He did not say "sins," but "sin." The sin of the world takes in this dark inheritance which makes men go astray. How we rejoice that Christ can take it away!

This same removal of sin was typified in the Old Testament in one of the sacrifices for sin. It will be recalled by the reader that two goats were brought to the altar; one was slain and the blood used; while over the head of the second goat the

sins of the people were confessed and the animal
led away into the wilderness with this imposed
spiritual burden. In this symbolic scene we read
that while the blood has been shed for our sins,
there remains another act of grace in which iniquity is taken away.

Recently in our reading we came across the testimony of George Fox, the famous Quaker. His
experience is in delightful agreement with the argument made under this third point. We copy
his exact words: '' I knew Jesus, and he was precious to my soul; but I found something within
me that would not keep sweet and patient and
kind. I did what I could to keep it down, but it
was there. I besought Jesus to do something for
me, and when I gave him my will, he came to my
heart and took out all that would not be sweet, all
that would not be kind, all that would not be patient, and then he shut the door.''

A fourth figure is that of destruction.

In Romans Paul tells us that the '' body of sin ''
is to be ''*destroyed*.'' And this is not to be done
at death, for he says immediately after that we
should no longer '' serve sin.'' It is to be done
in life, that we may present a holy and blameless
life to the world.

John also speaks to the point and says: "For this purpose the Son of God was manifested, that he might *destroy* the works of the devil."

The reader will notice that the word is not suppress, paralyze, or keep under, but *destroy*. A letter or book destroyed is the end of that article. Destruction means destruction. Free moral agency is not destroyed; no moral power or susceptibility of the soul is annihilated, but the proneness to sin, the body of sin, the "old man," is destroyed. God created moral powers and susceptibilities within us, while the devil implanted a bias or proneness to sin. Christ has not come to destroy the works of God, but the works of the devil.

Is it not amazing that we have men in the pulpit to-day, posing as religious teachers and expounders of God's Word, who affirm that the sin principle, or body of sin, remains through life, and that in the face of the express declaration of the Bible?

Paul is not referring to the deathbed scene or hour when he speaks of the crucifixion of the "old man" and the destruction of the body of sin. The proof of this is that he affirms that by this destruction we are placed where henceforth we should not "serve sin." This shows that he is speaking of the life on earth, and not that in heaven. And we have his additional words: "Now, being made free from sin, and become servants to God, ye have your fruit unto holiness, and the end everlasting life."

Reason itself demands that this deliverance from sin should take place in time. The honor of Christ demands it. What a belittling of the Saviour and his redemption it would be, if we were compelled to say that the nature of sin could not be removed by his power! How his work would suffer in contrast with that of the devil, who wrought a harm and curse in the soul that Christ is unable to uplift and undo!

The safety of the soul demands this destruction to take place in life. The mercy of God has determined that it shall be done, and, thank God, by the power of the Son of God it is done.

It is wonderful how the soul recognizes this peculiar destructive work. It is felt to be different from that wrought in conversion. Regeneration is life-giving and constructive, but sanctification is destructive and death-dealing. Something is felt to be taken away—yes, destroyed—when the blessing comes upon us. Bishop Hamline speaks of the divine work as "a holy, sin-consuming energy."

A lady in Tennessee, looking upward and praying for the blessing, suddenly received it, and in describing the experience said that something was taken out, and something came in.

The wife of a minister in Arkansas leaped to her feet as the holy fire fell upon her soul, crying out in an ecstasy: " The ' old man ' is dead! the ' old man ' is dead! "

Certainly it stands to reason that if we feel painfully the presence of this principle of evil, we shall most delightfully realize its removal and absence.

We have the witness of our own spirits to this destruction of the " old man." Besides this, we have the witness of the Word, which declares that the body of sin is destroyed. And clearer still we have the witness of the Holy Spirit, who, in a delightful, indescribable language of his own, thrills the soul with the testimony of the fact. Who is it that says there is no specific witness of the Spirit to sanctification? Let such a one turn to Hebrews x. 14, 15, and hear what the Book says: " For by one offering he hath perfected forever them which are sanctified. Whereof the Holy Ghost also is a witness to us."

12

CHAPTER XVII.

SUCH a deliverance as that described in the foregoing chapter implies a way of obtainment. Being a divine work and deliverance, it is not an attainment, but an obtainment.

The way of approach to such a blessing should be simple. Reason and mercy alike cry out for a simple way. The fact of unlettered multitudes, the greater fact of the spiritual misery of these multitudes, and their craving for and need of such a blessing, would suggest the thought that God would not lay down an obscure and difficult way, but one that the simple-minded and the soul-burdened could easily discover and walk therein.

Here is the trouble with many to-day: that they look for profound scholarship and mighty intellectual gifts as the necessary condition of the understanding and obtainment of this grace; when, if this were the condition, the great mass of mankind would at the first count be ruled out.

So far from being apparent to the wise, it is "hidden from the wise." Not that a wise man cannot receive this blessing, but it is not to be

(178)

found in the lines of an earthly wisdom. The
mere reasoner will never see it. The precious secret is not discoverable through syllogisms. Logic
is utterly helpless at a door that opens only to another touch altogether.

A gentleman said to the author that reasoning
was perfectly allowable in the matter because God
himself said: "Come, now, and let us reason together." Our reply was that God said come reason together with *him*. It is not *human* reasoning,
a mental contest of man with man, that is alluded
to, but a conference with God. We all know that
reasoning with God will bring us most rapidly to
silence, tears, and the blood of the Lord Jesus
Christ. In addition to this the very substance of
this famous reasoning is given: "Though your
sins be as scarlet, they shall be as white as snow;
though they be red like crimson, they shall be as
wool!" Would that all reasoning were equally
blessed, and worthy to be remembered.

The way to the great deliverance ought to be
simple, then, if for no other reason than the goodness of God. Besides this, the way must be simple because of the great multitude of people who
cannot obtain the blessing in any other manner.
The way, thank God, is simple.

Two steps or compliances on our part will bring us to the point where God will destroy the " old man " and give us a pure heart. These two steps are consecration and faith.

The conditions of justification and regeneration are repentance and faith. We see no mention made of consecration, from the fact that the sinner has nothing to consecrate. He *surrenders*, which, to the hasty glance, looks like consecration, but it is not the same. It is human wisdom that has tacked on consecration as a condition of pardon. The Bible itself says repent and believe, and we shall be saved.

But to the pardoned and regenerated man comes the words of Paul in Romans xii. 1, 2: " I beseech you, brethren, . . . present your bodies a living sacrifice." The result, he says, will be a " transformation," a " renewing," a " proving the will of God," which will, he tells us in Thessalonians, is " even your sanctification."

If a man desires the blessing spoken of in this volume, the first step to be taken is

CONSECRATION.

Present all to God. Keep back nothing. Let there be no mental reservation. Let body, soul, talents, time, will, reputation, property, family, and everything, be laid on the altar.

This is what we owe to God. It is our reasonable service. It is what all have to do sooner or later. Death compels us to give up all to God— body, spirit, friends, land, home, and all. As a compulsory act it brings no blessing. But if we do it voluntarily, the blessed experience of sanctification is the result.

Let not the reader stop to speculate and doubt, but test the matter faithfully for himself. It is worth a faithful trial; yes, verily, a thousand trials.

Some have received the light and rejoice in the deliverance. Let their assurance reassure the reader of these lines. It is true. Only do as bidden by the word of God and by the great crowd of rejoicing witnesses in the land, and the seeker will become the finder, and know for himself beyond all doubt the truth of these things we have written.

The second step is

FAITH.

Believe that God accepts the consecration; that our altar, which Paul says is Christ, sanctifies the gift thus laid upon the altar, and sanctifies it *now*.

Do not say, " I feel it," or, " I know it," until the witness comes; but say, "*I believe it.*" Feeling is one thing, knowledge is another, and faith a third. Neither feeling nor knowledge is expected of us at this time, but simply faith.

We are required to believe God's word, and that word says: " The altar sanctifieth the gift." God cannot and will not sanctify unbelief. Man wandered from God and fell through doubt of his word; he is to come back through belief of the truth, by an unshaken confidence in every word.

Here are some of God's words: " Whatsoever toucheth the altar shall be holy," " The altar sanctifieth the gift." Faith must take hold of and rest on these statements of God. The result will come speedily, and be most wonderful and satisfactory.

These are the two steps. In taking them, however, there is another exercise of the soul which accompanies both steps—viz.,

PRAYER.

Consecration and faith are the conditions of obtaining sanctification; yet neither one will be born or continue to live without prayer. Through prayer we gather strength to consecrate, and through prayer faith is aroused and stimulated to take hold of the great blessing.

The disciples had been praying for ten days when the baptism of fire suddenly fell upon them. For three days the writer was living in supplication, every breath was a petition, when swiftly, graciously, overwhelmingly, the blessing sought after, consecrated for, believed in, and prayed for, came upon his soul.

Our advice to every seeker of sanctification is: Live upon your knees. Pray whether you feel like it or not. Pray with words and without words. Pray with groanings that cannot be uttered. Let your sighs be prayers. Sometimes we never pray more acceptably and prevailingly than when stretched on our faces, we groan for deliverance before God. Knock on and call at the door of mercy until the very noise will create remark in heaven. The kingdom suffereth violence, and the King is well pleased with importunity. The inevitable result of all this will be the descending baptism of fire, and the clear, unmistakable witness of the Spirit to the sanctification of the soul.

When the witness comes we need not that any man should teach us what has happened. The soul is thrilled with the purifying work and the testifying Spirit. We know that inbred sin is gone and that the heart is pure.

Here is the time of shouts, overflowing gladness, radiant smiles, joyous laughter, happy tears,
or a great still peace according to the tempera-
ment of the individual. This is what the seeker
wanted to experience at the first, but which cannot possibly take place until the last. It is never
to be worked up, but comes spontaneously the instant the Holy Spirit witnesses to the accomplished work in the soul. We do not have to
work it up; it works itself up. It may come like
a cyclone, or it may be breathed on the heart as
gently as an evening zephyr from the South; but
in either case the soul will know perfectly well
what has happened, and will rejoice accordingly.

This, then, is the order of the work of grace:

> The Word Preached,
> Conviction for Inbred Sin,
> Prayer,
> Consecration,
> Continued Prayer,
> Faith,
> The Divine Instantaneous Work,
> The Witness of the Spirit,
> The Soul's Knowledge,
> The Feeling,
> Established.

The two great facts that produce the knowledge in the soul's consciousness of entire sanctification are the work of the Spirit and the witness of the Spirit. The soul is conscious of the change and hears the voice.

Then comes the feeling; then establishment.

Some critics may find fault with the fourth feature (Consecration), saying that we consecrate to obtain pardon. But the Bible does not say so, but states that the conditions of pardon are repentance and faith. What the critic takes to be the consecration of the sinner is, as stated in a previous chapter, nothing but surrender. The sinner surrenders; the Christian consecrates.

Furthermore, we would say that while a spirit of consecration is seen in every regenerated life that is worthy of the name, yet consecration is one thing and *perfect* consecration another; just as sanctification is seen to be one thing and entire sanctification something far deeper, sweeter, and more blessed. It is *perfect* consecration that secures *entire* sanctification.

The reader will also observe that the word "repentance" is not found in the order named above. The blessing held up here is for the Christian, and the real Christian should have nothing to repent of. He should, by virtue of the regenerated life, be living without sin, according to Bible statement. St. John, in his first Epistle, writes that it is while the child of God is walking in the light as God is in the light, and while having fellowship with his brethren, that the blessing comes down upon him and the blood of Christ cleanseth from *all* sin.

Repentance presupposes a sinful and backslidden life, but the blessing of sanctification is for the soul that is in a justified condition and walking in the clear light with a joyous sense of acceptance with God. There can be a profound conviction over the presence of inbred sin, with intense yearning for its removal, but this is not repentance.

Christ distinctly said that he had not come to call the righteous, but sinners, to repentance. But he did not say that he did not have a call for believers. On the contrary, the Bible says that "God has called us to holiness." Any one who reads the Epistles will recognize this call running throughout them all. And we confess to astonishment that men who are quick to see the call to repentance fail to observe the distinct call to holiness. Sinners are not called to holiness, but to repentance;

and Christians are not called to repentance, but to holiness. God " commands " sinners everywhere to repent, but he " beseeches " his people to present themselves upon the altar as a living sacrifice, holy and acceptable unto him.

Would that Christians everywhere that have not the blessing spoken of in this volume would put themselves under full salvation preaching. Soon inbred sin, or the plague of the heart, would be revealed, and deep conviction would take place. Prayer, consecration, and faith would swiftly follow. Then would come the baptism of fire purifying the heart, and the delightful witness of the Holy Ghost to the work. Knowledge of the work at once would fill the mind, joy overflow the heart, and the life, settled and grounded upon Christ, enter upon a restful experience that language cannot satisfactorily describe.

As we know what blessedness the death of the " old man " or sanctification is to the individual, and what power and glory and victory it means to the Church, we cannot but breathe the prayer of the Psalmist: " O that the *salvation of Israel* were come out of Zion! when the Lord bringeth back the captivity of his people, Jacob shall rejoice, and Israel shall be glad.''

CHAPTER XVIII.

SCRIPTURE SUPPOSED TO TEACH THE IMPOSSIBILITY
OF POSSESSING A PURE HEART.

THERE are some in our midst who deny the possibility of a pure heart and holy life.

Such denials are in direct contradiction to the teaching of the Word of God, and show a profound ignorance of the plain statements that "whosoever is born of God doth not commit sin," and "whosoever abideth in him sinneth not." Such speeches bring into contempt the blessed work of the Son of God, who came to destroy the works of the devil, and make to mean nothing the words of the angel about him, that he would save his people from their sins. The plan of human redemption thus becomes a farce, and the word "salvation" itself is but an empty sound and mockery.

The Bible is called the Holy Bible, it came from a Holy God, shows the way to obtain a holy heart, live a holy life, and finally reach a holy heaven. There is not a single hint in it that God will allow us to sin; and while the atonement provides for the recovery of one who falls into sin, it does not pro-

vide for a man's sinning. It contemplates the res-
toration, and not the falling, of man ; the holiness,
and not the sinfulness, of the soul.   Hence every
commandment forbids sin, and every precept and
command and prayer points to holiness.

This being the case, it is certainly astonishing
to hear men plead for the privilege of sinning
some, deny the possibility of constantly living a
holy life, and in so doing convict God of cruelty
or folly.   For if God commands us to be holy, and
we cannot become so, then the command origi-
nates either in folly or cruelty.   There is no escape from this conclusion.

The objectors and deniers of the sanctified life
intrench themselves behind certain passages of
Scripture, which they quote in proof of their position.   We call attention to several.

The first is Proverbs xx. 9: "Who can say, I
have made my heart clean?"

We quickly reply: No one that we have ever
heard of but a madman.   Who could say such a
thing: "*I* have made my heart clean" The emphasis, laid upon the fourth word of the verse, " I "
unlocks the meaning of the verse, and shows that
the writer is declaring what we all will agree to:
the inability of a man to purify himself.   But while

we cannot do this work, another can; and while we
have never heard any man say that he had made
his heart clean, we have known myriads to declare
that *Christ* had done so.   This is certainly a very
different thing.

A second verse is Ecclesiastes vii. 20: " For
there is not a just man upon earth, that doeth
good, and sinneth not."

This passage is felt to be very strong by the objectors, and is quoted with smiles of certain tri-
umph.   But the seeming strength of the verse
arises from an improper translation.   No less a
Bible critic and scholar than Dr. Adam Clarke
calls attention to the fact that the mood in which
the verb appears in the original is not made to appear in the King James version, and that the true
reading is: " There is not a just man upon earth
that doeth good and may not sin."

With this fact we all heartily agree; we firmly
believe in the possibility of sinning while in the
body on probation.   If a good man fell in Eden,
a good man may fall outside of Eden, and in his
home and in the Church.   No well balanced holiness teacher ever says that we cannot sin, but declares instead that while we may sin, yet, thank
God, through Christ we need not.   " I cannot

sin " is a speech that belongs to the fair land and country beyond the grave, while " I can, but do not sin " is an utterance that we are privileged beyond question to utter in this life.

A third quotation is made from 1 Kings viii. 46 and 2 Chronicles vi. 36. They are identical. " If they sin against thee (for there is no man that sinneth not)."

The explanation is that there is the same failure to bring out the proper mood, which when done we have the words: " for there is no man that may not sin."

A striking confirmation of this meaning is seen in the word " if."   " If they sin " shows that possibly they may not, and anyhow need not. For how silly it would be to say: "*If* they sin—for there is no man that sinneth not."   It is seen that the two sentences thus arrayed against each other make an absurd statement.

So we are doubly driven to the true rendering, " If they sin against thee (for there is no man that may not sin)."

A fourth verse cited is Matthew xix. 17: "And he [*i. e.*, Christ] said unto him, Why callest thou me good? there is none good but one, that is, God."

This is regarded by some as containing a Waterloo defeat to the advocates of a sanctified experience and life. The slightest glance will show their mistake.

Christ was speaking here about the Father. According to the objectors then he ruled himself out and said that he, the Son, was not good. Such a construction of his words proves too much, as they say in logic, and so proves nothing if forced in that way.

What kind of goodness was he talking about? Any thoughtful person will say absolute goodness. He was affirming that there was only one being who possessed underived goodness, in whom goodness dwelt inherently and from all eternity. In that sense there is none good but one, and that is God. But while this is so, he does not teach that there cannot be relative goodness, and that a soul coming to God may not be filled to overflowing with divine goodness. Nor does his gospel teach that men have not been thus filled, and that there are no good men. On the contrary, the Bible says that Barnabas "was a good man, and full of the Holy Ghost," and so of others.

A fifth passage is Romans iii. 10: "There is none righteous, no, not one."

The trouble with people who quote such passages as this is that they do not read the context, the verses going before and coming after. If they did, they would be surprised to see the meaning that they had first attached to the passages utterly vanish away.

Let the reader turn to Romans iii. 10, and then continue reading, and have his eyes opened, that the Lord was not speaking here of his people at all, as the description that follows proves.

"There is none that understandeth, there is none that seeketh after God."

Why surely this is not a description of everybody, for we all know many people who do understand and seek after God.

"Their throat is an open sepulcher; . . . the poison of asps is under their lips."

The writer knows many Christians who have no such throats and no such poisonous lips.

"Whose mouth is full of cursing."

There are people reading these lines who never did, and never will curse.

"Their feet are swift to shed blood."

Countless millions of people have never committed murder.

"The way of peace they have not known."

13

Behold, we could not count the multitudes in different Churches who know all about, and daily and hourly enjoy, the way of peace.

Does it not dawn upon the reader that here is not a description of God's people at all, but of one of Satan's crowds. To think of such a company thrusting its own photograph before the eyes of the Lord's redeemed and saying: " Look at your picture!" What amazing impudence and ignorance is here seen!

The passage is recognized by commentators as a picture of depravity, or the condition of the soul without the regenerating and sanctifying grace of God; but none of them supposed or taught that these corrupt hearts, sepulchered throats, and poisonous lips, could not be cleansed and made to glorify God thereafter with holy hearts and lives.

A sixth quotation is from Romans iii. 23: " For all have sinned, and come short of the glory of God."

This is true—no one dreams of denying it. We believe that every man has sinned in the past. The statement of the verse is in regard to the past. We have all sinned in the years that are gone. But that is no reason why we should sin in the days and years to come. We once transgressed through ignorance and unbelief, but through belief and knowledge of the truth, which makes us clean and free, we can, according to God's word, live soberly, righteously, and godly in this present world.

A seventh citation is 1 John i. 8: "If we say that we have no sin, we deceive ourselves, and the truth is not in us."

Here is another formidable-looking verse, that at first glance seems to call for an Appomattox surrender on the part of the holiness people; but with a little fixed attention, and by reading the context, the whole passage becomes clear.

In the first place, let the reader remember that John is writing to Christians, and that he has said to them in this same Epistle that "whosoever is born of God, sinneth not," and that he urges this upon them again in the words: "These things write I unto you, that ye sin not."

The question we urge now is: How can Christians find excuse for sin in the face of such statements? How can the reader reconcile these verses with a life of sin? Evidently the passage advanced by the objectors must refer to something else, or we have established the startling fact that the word of God contradicts itself. Here we read that we must not sin, and yet if we say that we have no sin we deceive ourselves.　What is the explanation? There is one, and one that should commend itself to any unprejudiced mind.

The Bible throughout recognizes two kinds of sin, a fact that the Churches have embodied in their creeds and articles of religion, calling one personal or actual sin, and the other inbred, inherited, or original sin.　One is an act; the other is a nature. One is a transaction; the other, a bias or principle.

Being so diverse, they are described differently and are treated differently.　The dissimilarity is made evident by distinguishing terms of quite a variety.　One way of discrimination appears in this chapter in the words " sin " and " sins."　Nor is it the only place by any means where this peculiar discrimination is observed.　David in the fifty-first Psalm, and Paul in his Epistles, both recognize this difference in sin, and use language accordingly.

" Sin " stands for the inherited principle or nature, while " sins " refer to our personal transgressions.　Both of these words appear in the first chapter of John's Epistle.　" If we confess our *sins*, he is faithful and just to forgive us our *sins*." Again: " If we walk in the light, as he is in the light, .　.　.　the blood of Jesus Christ his Son cleanseth us from all *sin!* "

That two different kinds of sin, and two different works, are referred to here appears in the use of the singular and plural numbers by way of contrast. And also that in one case the man is in an unforgiven state and comes confessing his sins; in the other, the person is walking in the light *as God is in the light.* In the one, the man is pardoned; in the other case the man is cleansed, and cleansed while walking in the light. One obtains deliverance from " sins;" the other, from " sin."

According to these facts, a regenerated man, or one born of God, has been forgiven of his *"sins"* (plural number), but sin (singular number) in the form of inbred sin is still left. If such a man should say that he is without " sin" (and many are saying it to-day who deny sin left in the regenerated heart), he deceiveth himself. The thing to do is, after we have confessed our " sins " and been forgiven, to walk in the light as He is in the light, having fellowship one with another, and right there in the light of a blessed regenerated life we shall suddenly be cleansed from *all* " sin."

Thus being forgiven of " sins " and cleansed from " sin," who wonders that John writes: " These things write I unto you, that ye sin not? "

The eighth passage cited is Proverbs xxiv. 16:

'' For a just man falleth seven times, and riseth up again.''

We call attention to the fact that this verse is usually quoted in this remarkable way: '' For a good man sinneth seven times a day!'' It is said that the devil never quotes the Scripture correctly. The devil is not alone in that particular. Standing in a hotel one day we heard a man of the world, who was laughing at the idea of holiness, say: '' What can be expected of a man like myself, when the Bible says: 'A good man *sinneth* seven times *a day?*'' '' We Italicize the words that are not God's words. The real verse reads differently: '' A good man falleth seven times, and riseth up again.''

We are glad to notice in the first place that we do not have to fall seven times a day. This is certainly in itself a great relief. The thought of seven falls in a lifetime, sad as it is, is more endurable than the seven daily overtakings and overwhelmings.

In the second place, we are delighted to find on tracing the word '' falleth '' back into the original that it does not mean sin at all, but refers to temporal affliction or trouble. So the true meaning of the verse is that a just man will or may fall into great sorrows or troubles seven times in his life, but he shall rise up from them all!

So ends the boasted array of Scripture that was supposed to teach the impossibility of being pure in heart and holy in life. The false meanings attributed to them go down before an honest investigation, and especially before the heavy broadsides of the Ten Commandments and such cannonades as "Stand in awe and *sin not*," "Awake to righteousness and *sin not*." "These things write I unto you, that ye *sin not*."

To crown all, after we go over the battlefield and make a closer scrutiny of these scriptural batteries that were supposed to be firing into us and our claims concerning holiness we discover that they are our own guns, and are really pointing against the men who have tried to use them against us, and that they are in perfect harmony with the rest of the Bible, which teaches us the gracious fact that God has granted to us through the life and death of his Son that " we, being delivered out of the hand of our enemies, might serve him without fear, in holiness and righteousness before him, all the days of our life."

CHAPTER XIX.

THE opposers of the doctrine of a second work subsequent to regeneration, realizing that their simple denial of the truth will not be sufficient, but that a thus saith the Lord is properly demanded of them, have been at pains to produce certain scriptures which they affirm ring the death-knell of the doctrine.

One of the passages most frequently quoted by them is Philippians iii. 12–14: "Not as though I had already attained, either were already perfect. . . . I count not myself to have apprehended," etc. This is brought forward to show that Paul never claimed the blessing of sanctification or Christian perfection; that instead he herein plainly denies it in the words "not attained," "not perfect," and "not apprehended."

We confess to amazement at such an interpretation. Let the reader look at the entire paragraph, and see for himself what the apostle was talking about.

"If by any means I might *attain* unto the *resurrection of the dead*. Not as though I had already *attained*, either were already perfect: but I follow after, if that I may apprehend that for which also I am apprehended of Christ Jesus. Brethren, I count not myself to have apprehended: but this one thing I do, forgetting those things which are behind, and reaching forth unto those things which are before, I press toward the mark for the prize of the high calling of God in Christ Jesus. *Let us therefore, as many as be perfect*, be thus minded."

Several facts become clear to the honest inquirer:

First, there are two perfections mentioned in the passage; one, Paul said he had; the other, he had not. The one in the twelfth verse he said he did not possess; the one in the fifteenth verse he said he had.

Secondly, in the first " perfection " or " attainment " he was not speaking of sanctification, but of the resurrection of the dead. The eleventh and twelfth verses settle the fact beyond all question.

Thirdly, the word " attained " is used in connection with the word " resurrection," " If by any means I might *attain* unto the resurrection of the dead." So the apostle could not be speaking here of sanctification.

Fourthly, when he says in the twelfth verse that he was not "already perfect" he was again speaking of the glorified state, of the life beyond the grave. The literal translation is: "Not that I have already been perfected." The marginal reference is Hebrews xii. 23, which proves that he was speaking of the heavenly state. Dr. Adam Clarke says that Paul here "alluded not to deficiency of grace, but to his martyrdom."

Fifthly, the word "apprehended" is found in the same verse, and in such close connection with the word "attain" that any one can see that he was still speaking of the life and glory to be had with Christ in the glorified state. Moreover, the word itself gives light. "Apprehend" here means to "lay hold." But sanctification cannot be laid hold of, but is a grace and condition wrought within us by another hand altogether. A man may lay hold of a martyr's crown and its rewards, but not of sanctification. God lays hold of us there.

Sixthly, the word "prize," in the fourteenth verse, shows us that he was not speaking of Christian perfection. "I press toward the mark for the prize." Sanctification is not a prize. Heaven, eternal life, celestial rewards, are prizes; but holiness is a privilege, a duty, a condition, a blessed means to an end, and the way itself to the attainment of the " prize."

Seventhly, the word " attained " proves that the apostle was not speaking of sanctification. This word alone can settle the question, and in this way: That sanctification is never presented in the Bible as an attainment, but as an obtainment. The words are very different. There are two ways of coming into possession of a fortune. One is to labor and save up for it; the other is to inherit it. The first takes years; the second occurs in a moment. One is an attainment; the other, an obtainment. The Christian can, by a life of devotedness to Christ, attain unto distinctive and superior rewards in the resurrection, but no one can by any amount of religious work attain unto the blessing of holiness. Sanctification is always an obtainment of grace through faith in the Lord Jesus Christ. The word " attain" then shows that Paul was not speaking of sanctification.

Eighthly, the fifteenth verse puts the matter beyond peradventure in the following words: "Let us therefore, as many *as be perfect*, be thus minded." Could anything be clearer? Paul, in the beginning of the paragraph, disclaims glorified perfection, and says that he is pressing after it; but there is another perfection which he does claim. This is the same perfection that he urges the Christian Hebrews to " go on to," and which John, in his Epistle, calls " perfect love," and Mr. Wesley calls Christian perfection.

A preacher once took issue with me in this interpretation in the following language: " What folly and absurdity it is to make Paul say that he was striving and pressing forward for the resurrection of the dead, when it is well known that we will be raised from the dead, no matter whether we strive or not! "

The preacher overlooked a fact that to-day is thrilling many scholarly Christian minds. It was not the general resurrection Paul was talking about, but a peculiar one, *a resurrection from among the dead!* The overlooked preposition " ek " gives this gracious and yet startling light. There is to be a resurrection a thousand years before the general resurrection. It is to be out from among the dead. Some will arise, and many will sleep on. A certain grace and life will secure this early and glorious arising. Paul said that he was after that, pressing forward for that, and " Let us therefore, as many as *be perfect*, be thus *minded*."

A second verse relied on to disprove a second

work is 2 Corinthians v. 17: " Therefore if any
man be in Christ, he is a new creature: old things
are passed away; behold, all things are become
new."

One point made by the opposers from this verse
is that a new creature must necessarily be a sound
and perfect creature.

Our reply is that this does not follow, for such
is not the case in nature or grace. An earthly
child is a new creature, but it is often born with
inherited disease. So with the child of God. He
is by conversion a new creature; but he has a dark
inheritance which speedily discovers itself after
regeneration in forms of doubt, pride, envy, impa-
tience, uncharitableness, and other disturbing
things. He is a new creature, but not a pure
creature. The two expressions are not synonymous.

A second point made by the opposers is that the
verse declares " all things are become new; "
that, according to this statement, no inbred sin is
left, and so nothing remains to require a second
work, and therefore the doctrine must fall through.

To this we reply that, if *all things* are become
new in regeneration, why is it that only a few
verses farther on Paul begins a chapter with an

exhortation to these same regenerated people, whom he calls " babes in Christ," and hence born of God, and bids them cleanse themselves from " all *filthiness* of the flesh and *spirit*."

Again, some things never become new. We have God's own statement that " the carnal mind is enmity against God: for it is not subject to the law of God, *neither indeed can be*." Besides this, the " old man " is never said to become a New Man. The " old man " *dies*, and then the New Man clothes us. So, to force this verse, in the expression " all things are become new," to include the regeneration or renewing of the " old man " is to make God contradict himself.

To crown all, the Revised Version leaves out the word " all," and we have the verse: " Old things are passed away; behold, they are become new."

This, indeed, is what we felt at conversion. Old things did pass away; there seemed to us a newness, sweetness, freshness, gladness, in everything; yet after that we found the " old man " left in the heart. He never becomes new; he is under sentence of death to be " crucified " and " destroyed."

A third quotation by the opposers is 1 Peter i.

22, 23: "Seeing ye have purified your souls in obeying the truth through the Spirit unto unfeigned love of the brethren, see that ye love one another with a pure heart fervently: being born again, not of corruptible seed, but of incorruptible, by the word of God, which liveth and abideth forever."

The argument based on this verse is: How can anything corrupt be in a being born of incorruptible seed?

We reply that, if the new birth saves us from the presence of indwelling corruption, how is it that two verses after Peter begs these same people to lay aside " all malice, and all guile, and all hypocrisies, and envies, and all evil speakings," and "as *newborn* babes, desire the sincere milk of the word?" This last verse unanswerably demonstrates the existence of remaining sin in the regenerated heart; for here is asserted the fact of their being " newborn," while the sins mentioned are all heart sins. The " laying aside " refers to that perfect consecration, that close approach to God, that sanctifying of self which precedes the sanctifying work of the Spirit.

As to the argument built on the words " Seeing ye have purified your souls in obeying the truth," and "See that ye love one another with a pure heart fervently," we make answer that this could hardly be the blessing of entire sanctification, for only a few verses preceding the apostle exhorts them to that blessing in the words: "Be ye holy." Besides, he says: "Ye have purified your souls." In entire sanctification God does the purifying. Moreover, genuinely sanctified people hardly need to be told to love one another; for when filled with perfect love they cannot help loving one another fervently.

A fourth verse brought against us is 1 John v. 18: "We know that whosoever is born of God sinneth not; but he that is begotten of God keepeth himself, and that wicked one toucheth him not."

The argument drawn from this passage is that there is no need of a second work of grace to keep us from sinning; that if born of God we sin not, and this itself is a pure and holy life.

Our reply is that we have never asserted that we need sanctification to keep us from sinning; regeneration alone can do that. The work of sanctification goes deeper, and takes the "prone to wander" and "want to sin" out of us. Regeneration saves us from the guilt and power of sin, but sanctification delivers us from the inbeing of sin.

A fifth verse urged against the second work is James iii. 11: " Doth a fountain send forth at the same time sweet water and bitter?"

The argument formed from the above is that there should be nothing contrary to holiness in the child of God. God has sweetened the waters of his life, how can they be bitter?

Our reply is that there is nothing wrong with the water of life, but the trouble is with something left in the regenerated heart that gives the occasional bitterness to word and act.

James denies that such a state of things exists in nature, but affirms that it is seen in the spiritual life. He tries to shame Christians with this very fact: that they are seen doing what is not according to nature. No fountain sends out sweet and bitter water, and yet here among you, he says, " Out of the same mouth proceedeth blessing and cursing" (scolding). Then adds: " My brethren, these things ought not so to be."

Furthermore, both observation and experience agree in proof that the regenerated heart is a fountain from which proceeds sweet and bitter water. O the blessings and scoldings we have

14

heard come from the lips of the same child of God! The trouble is inbred sin. Get that sanc-tified out, and the fountain will run pure and sweet all the time.

We confess to surprise that any one should quote this verse from James as if he had said that there could not be sweet and bitter streams from the same heart, when this is the very thing he affirms, and says it is in the " brethren." " My brethren, these things ought not so to be."

Truly it ought not to be so, for sanctification can end it.

A sixth passage relied on by the opposition is Matthew vii. 17, 18: " Every good tree bringeth forth good fruit; but a corrupt tree bringeth forth evil fruit. A good tree cannot bring forth evil fruit, neither can a corrupt tree bring forth good fruit.''

The argument made here by our brethren against us is that a regenerated man does right and the sinner does wrong; that a Christian is a good tree, and cannot and does not bear corrupt fruit; that he is sound to the heart; and there is, therefore, no corruption remaining in him.

The simple reply that punctures all this is the question: Where does the corruption come from that we see in the lives of regenerated people? Does the good tree that Christ planted in their hearts bring forth such fruit as ambition, pride, ill will, suspicion, evil speaking, irritability, fear of man, lust, and love of the world?

The whole mistake of the opposition springs from the failure to recognize that there are *two trees* in the heart, a good tree planted by Christ, and a corrupt tree planted by Satan and called inbred sin or depravity, under the shadow of which we are born into the world. Until Christ planted the tree of life, or regeneration, there was only evil fruit in the man's soul. But after that beautiful planting men came and gathered from the greensward of our lives the strangest mixture of sweet and bitter, good and evil fruit. Christ touches his heavenly plant, and lo! a shower of golden celestial fruit in our thoughts, words, and actions; another time Satan shakes his tree, and alas! there comes tumbling down upon the hands and heads of the people a dark and bitter fruitage from another world altogether. The way to do is to have inbred sin, or the corrupt tree, cut down as is done in sanctification, and then the pure, unmixed fruit of holiness will abound to the good of man and the glory of God.

A seventh citation is 1 Corinthians ix. 27: " But
I keep under my body, and bring it into subjection:
lest that by any means, when I have preached to
others, I myself should be a castaway."

The argument made from this passage is that
repression of sin is all that can be hoped for in the
Christian life. That sin cannot be extirpated, but
must be kept under; that we need not expect to
be better than Paul, and yet here is a statement
from him to the effect that he had always to be
keeping his sinful flesh under and so bring it into
subjection.

This whole plausible speech is utterly swept
away by calling attention to a fact plainly appearing in the Bible—viz., that the word " body " stands
for one thing and the word " flesh " for another.
In the verse quoted above Paul uses the word *soma*,
meaning the human body; but in Galatians v. 17,
when he says, " the flesh lusteth " he employs the
Greek word *sarx*, which, as stated in a previous
chapter, the apostle uses to describe carnality, a
fleshly principle apart from the body.

This being the case, a flood of light is poured on
both verses, as we see that they speak of different
things—one of the body, the other of the carnal
mind. The latter is to be " destroyed;" the for-

mer we are to " keep under." God has no quarrel with the body (*soma*), but with inbred sin (*sarx*). By the grace of God the " flesh " can be crucified and destroyed, and after this we simply watch over, keep under and in proper subjection the " body," with its natural appetites and inclinations.

It would be a mistake to kill a horse because he is wild; the thing to do is to get the wildness out of him; hitch him to a buggy, and then, reins in hand, drive, guide, and control him while he does his proper work.

In the Dark Ages men were maltreating and destroying their " bodies," thinking that these were referred to in the word " flesh." As in the case of the wild horse, so we say here that it is a pity and a mistake to destroy the human " body," because of the " flesh," carnality. The true course is laid down in the Bible; get the " flesh " crucified and destroyed, which has run away with the " body; " and then with that inward, disturbing principle gone, how easy it is to control and keep under the body! The " body " is God's creation; the " flesh " is the devil's work. When the " flesh " is gone, the " body " can render God, man, and the owner most blessed service. Then it is that

the " body " fairly bowls along to glory, only re-
quiring, as in the case of the well tamed horse, the
controlling and directing eye and hand.

The eighth quotation is 1 Corinthians xv. 31: " I
die daily."

This language of Paul is brought forward to disprove the instantaneous and final death of inbred
sin, which we assert is taught in the Word of God
and verified in Christian experience.   You claim,
they say, to die once; but Paul said, " I die daily."

Here again the slightest attention to words brings
clear light and explanation.   Paul said, "*I* die
daily; " he did not say that the " old man " died
daily.   The " old man " has his moment of death
and is cast out of the soul.   There is no experience
clearer to the human heart than the fact of the
death of inbred sin.   The Spirit witnesses to it,
the soul rejoices in it.   But distinct from this is a
daily death that awaits the sanctified in this world.
Not a death of agony such as we had in the seeking and reception of the blessing of sanctification;
but the application of this same death to daily sur-
roundings and new circumstances that will constantly arise.   Trials, temptations, favors, friend-
ships, promotions, praises, flatteries, cuts, insults,
wrongs, persecutions, and countless other expe-

riences will come into the life; but with the " old man " out and the New Man in, the sanctified soul accepts each one as the Saviour would have him, and so dies to them all. To the world it looks like a daily death, and the man himself so describes it, but it is not like the death of the " old man " fraught with intense suffering; there is in this daily dying an element of joy and a perpetual shout of victory.

The ninth Scripture used to combat and destroy the doctrine of the second work of grace is John xv. 3: "Now ye are clean through the word which I have spoken unto you."

The argument based on this is that Christ, in addressing his disciples as regenerated men, said that they were " clean; " that if clean, then they were not unclean; and if clean, what need for a further work? that, therefore, there is no room in our theology or experience for a second work of grace.

Our reply to this is that our disagreeing brethren fail to distinguish between personal cleanness, as a man stands before God as accountable to him as an individual, and an uncleanness in nature transmitted by birth for which the man is not responsible. For instance, a man's personal sins are one thing, and depravity, the effect of Adam's sin on the soul, is another. In justification and regeneration a man's individual transgressions are pardoned, his guilt washed away, the evil bent and injury that he has personally brought upon his own soul is rectified, and the life of God implanted. He stands personally clean before God, but there still remains in 'him that bias of the soul to evil wrought by Adam's fall and transmitted to him as a dark inheritance. This remaining nature is felt by every converted person and is recognized and grieved over as spiritual uncleanness. Thus it is that Christ can say to every regenerated man and woman, " Ye are clean," and yet inbred sin be left within them.

An additional convincing fact we bring forward as proof on this line, and which the objectors seem to have overlooked, is this: If the disciples were pure, as some contend, because Christ said, " Ye are clean," why is it that a few minutes afterwards he prayed the Father to " sanctify them?" Careful to quote the words " ye are clean," our brethren of the other side are strangely careless in overlooking the words that almost immediately followed, " Sanctify them." The word " sanctify" in the Greek means to make pure, to make holy.

This last prayer did not mean to " set apart"

these disciples to preach, heal, and cast out devils, for, according to Mark iii. 14, 15, this had been done three years before. It meant that they might receive that which afterwards came upon them on the day of Pentecost—namely, the baptism of the Holy Ghost and of fire—by which inbred sin is destroyed, the heart made pure, and the life holy.

The last verse we mention as quoted by the opposers to a second work is Proverbs iv. 18: "But the path of the just is as the shining light, that shineth more and more unto the perfect day."

The reader will at first hardly see how this passage can be twisted to bear against the doctrine of heart purity. The explanation is that the opposers of an instantaneous sanctification seem to think that when we affirm that there is a second and completing work of grace in the soul we teach a stoppage of Christian growth, a cessation of religious activity, a discarding of means of grace, and so sink into a kind of " Hindoo stillness " or lazy, self-satisfied, fanciful perfection.

With this mistaken view of what sanctification is and does for the soul, some have quoted the passage above as though it annihilated us, when we love that Scripture and believe in it as heartily as those who use it against us.

Perhaps if all classes of Christians were brought to the witness stand it would be found that the sanctified man enjoys the experience laid down in this verse even more than his regenerated brother. Certainly, if it describes any one, it is the soul that has been purified from inbred sin and is going on from glory to glory. We feel like appealing to the reader and asking him as in the presence of God if this quoted verse truly describes the regenerated man's experience? Does his path look like the shining light, and does it shine more and more? Is there a steady increase all the time of light, life, and power? Observation tells us that this is not so; that if the regenerated soul does not press on at once into perfection and holiness the path of the just gets darker and darker, and the end is coldness, formality, and backsliding.

There are ministers to-day in the pulpit using this verse against the doctrine of sanctification, whose own light has never been as bright as in the first year or month or day of their converted lives. And yet this Scripture calls for an experience that grows brighter all the time. There are thousands of backsliders in the Church whose paths grew dark and darker after the first few days of their regeneration until at last every beam went out of their spiritual skies, and they are now walking in the night once more. And yet this verse calls for an experience of ever increasing glory and brightness.

As we look at the passage again we feel sure that it can only be made to apply to two classes. One is the regenerated man pressing on to perfection; and of course his way will be " the path of the just " (or justified) " that shineth more and more unto the perfect day," the day when God's perfecting work is done, and perfect love fills the soul. The other class is the sanctified. Truly the life of the man whose life has been made pure grows brighter and brighter unto the perfect day that awaits the soul in heaven.

Summing up the thoughts in this chapter, we affirm that God has a second work for the soul that is a completing work; yet as a work it does not stop growth in grace, progress in knowledge, or advancement in the divine life. Regeneration removes personal sins and personal guilt; sanctification removes inherited or inbred sin; and this completes the direct work of salvation. But from that time on the child of God grows in grace more rapidly than before, adds every spiritual excellence and practice to the life; while his path grows brighter and still brighter unto the perfect day.

CHAPTER XX.

MUCH of the mental confusion and trouble existing in regard to the sanctified life arises, as suggested by the caption of this chapter, from ignorance of scriptural and religious terms. Take, for instance,

CONSECRATION AND SANCTIFICATION.

Here are two words different in appearance, different in meaning, with one referring to a duty of man, and the other to a work of God; and yet these words are being made to mean the same by multiplied thousands in the Church.

Joshua used the first in addressing the people of Israel: "Who then is willing to consecrate himself this day to the Lord." Paul uses the other word in his letter to the Thessalonians: "And the God of peace sanctify you wholly." Would that God's servants kept them as clearly apart to-day as did the inspired Paul and Heaven-directed Joshua. Some of our hymnologists have failed to see the difference in the words, and so one writes:

Consecrate me now to thy service, Lord.

(220)

We can never sing that line without a mental protest; for God can no more do our consecrating than he can our repenting.

To give the reader an idea of how this confusion of definition and scriptural meaning exists, we give a quotation from one of the leading preachers and editors in our Southern Church as it appeared recently in a religious paper. Let the reader see for himself how two totally different things are confounded by a teacher in Israel: " I am a firm believer in the doctrine of sanctification, but God's Word, if I read it aright, makes it an additional work of grace—an enlargement upon regeneration, in which soul, body, spirit, substance and all we have are placed upon God's altar for time and eternity. This is the sanctification I find in God's Word, profess and teach."

The youngest preacher in the itinerancy could tell this prominent minister that the above is nothing in the world but an act of consecration, and that consecration is no more sanctification than repentance is regeneration.

The writer quoted from says that " sanctification is an additional work of grace;" this we agree to; but he makes that additional work of grace to be simply an act of consecration, of himself and substance. God's work and God as a worker is completely left out. The man's act is made thus to be sanctification, when the Scripture says that Christ is " made unto us sanctification," and prays " the God of peace sanctify you." One verse alone out of many destroys the reasoning of the brother, a verse in which Jesus speaks and lifts sanctification out of the hands of man altogether, and lodges it outside of the man and distinct from his gifts and consecration; here it is: " The altar sanctifieth the gift."

Grace is never an act of man to God, but an act or work of God for and in man. So when we say that " sanctification is an additional work of grace," that sentence alone separates sanctification from human consecration, and puts the sanctifying power where it belongs and where it only resides—viz., in God.

For years the writer thought that a perfect consecration was the last and highest act and the profoundest experience to be enjoyed by the soul. So he went on beclouded in this regard, calling Church members to the altar, getting them to reconsecrate themselves, and noticing that in a few hours or days the whole work needed to be done over again. The emotion was gone, and the close walk with God was not to be seen as had been promised. Stability, steadfastness, or—to use a word which is not, but ought to be, in the dictionary—stickability was lacking.

The two words "consecration" and "sanctification" had not separated from one another, but shone on as one. There are binary suns in the firmament that reach us as one, but under the telescope they come apart and shine as two. The trouble in both cases is distance. So when we drew near to God and allowed the Holy Spirit to arouse and enlarge the view of heavenly things, suddenly, sweetly, delightfully we saw the two words, which had been heretofore as one, come apart and shine as two. Immediately several important discoveries were made. One was that consecration is not the last act of the soul in receiving holiness, nor is it the highest act. Faith comes after consecration, and is not only a later act in point of time, but a higher, grander act of the soul. Wonderful and blessed as it is to see a man give up self and all to God, yet this itself is outstripped when the man steps out on God's word and promise, and believes then and there that God makes him holy; that this blessing of purity that he had been seeking all his life unavailingly by growth or works is wrought in him instantaneously by the power of the blood of Jesus. Before this the man as a consecrator could measure up to many Bible worthies, but now as a believer, without a helpful sign about him, he joins company with Abraham, who walked out into empty space on the naked promise of Almighty God.

Another discovery at this time was that, sweet as is the state of conscious consecration, there is for the child of God a far deeper and higher experience that lies beyond consecration; and that experience is sanctification, or the destruction of the " old man."

Never shall we cease to thank God for these discoveries. They make a wonderful revolution in one's life. The valley of Baca, which has already become a well, will be still further blessed and become the land of Beulah. The Bible is from that time a new book; the Saviour a complete and constant Saviour; the life is kept hid in the secret place; the heart runs over with praises all the time; and the soul is " full of glory and of God."

O the difference between consecration and sanctification!

It is true that a sanctified man is a consecrated

man, but it is equally true that there is many a
consecrated person who is not sanctified, and does
not even believe in it.   The latter word is a larger
word, and means much more than the other.

That it is a larger word and means more and is
more is seen from the fact that we can be consecrated without being sanctified, but when sanctified we are always consecrated.   The lesser is in
the bosom of the greater.   That they are different
words is seen from the different treatment given
to the persons professing them.   The consecrated
man is despised by the world, while the sanctified
man is despised by the Church.   The consecrated
man is really popular in ecclesiastical circles, but
the sanctified man in the same circles is regarded
with sorrow, uneasiness, and disapproval.   Great
is the difference in the words and conditions.

It is true that the Bible says " Sanctify yourselves," but the next verses show that an external
cleansing mainly was referred to by Joshua, and
not the work of God which we are now writing
about in this book.

It is also true that Peter, writing to certain
churches, exhorted them to " sanctify the Lord
God " in their hearts.   But here again something
else is meant.   Dr. Clarke says that it is simply
    15

an entreaty that these people should entertain just and proper ideas of God.

Let us sum up.

Consecration is the duty and act of man; sanctification is the second gracious work of God in the soul. Consecration is a blessed attitude; sanctification is a holy state.

The joy of consecration arises from the consciousness of doing right and having given all to God; the joy of sanctification springs from a perpetual sense of purity, the abiding of perfect love in the heart, and the constant indwelling of the Saviour in the soul.

Grow; Go.

These words are different. The proof is found in the dictionary, by our use of them, and by their use and the meaning allotted to them in the Word of God.

And yet these two words, that are so distinctive and refer to such different things in the spiritual life, are confounded by many, and made synonymous.

Take the first word. Peter exhorts us to "grow" in grace. According to all observation of vegetable life a shrub or tree has to be *in* something to grow. It cannot grow to another soil or to a distant locality. It simply grows in a soil in which it is already planted.

So with the child of God. He has been planted through regeneration in the spiritual life, and is then told by the apostle to "grow *in*" that grace and life. There is no exhortation in the passage to strive for another, higher and distinct blessing, but to grow in the grace in which he finds himself.

There are two spiritual localities, so to speak, in the religious life. One is regeneration and the other sanctification. It is not more impossible for a tree to transport itself by growth from one clime to another than it is for the soul by mere growth in grace to pass from the regenerate to the sanctified state.

The tree grows where it is planted, but it requires a human hand to transport it from one place to another. So does the soul grow in grace and knowledge, but it takes the divine power to lift it from the grace of regeneration and plant it deeply and firmly in the grace and life of sanctification.

While in the regenerated life we grow; and when advanced into the sanctified life we continue to grow in grace; and when translated to the skies, still in heaven we will keep on growing in grace and knowledge.

Growth is the duty of man, and so he is commanded to grow. But no amount of growth on our part can ever accomplish a work that is in itself divine. We can never by any number of growing processes introduce or push ourselves into a state that is purely in itself the result of divine power.

Regeneration is a divine work; sanctification is a divine work; and the transporting of our souls and bodies into heaven is also the work of God. We may lop off our sins and all see the improvement; but reformation and improvement is not regeneration; and so God at last has to lift us into the regenerate state. Then we can grow in grace so rapidly that many will observe and admire; but growth in grace is not sanctification, and hence God has to lift us again, and this time into holiness. Then we can grow holier all the time; but all the holiness in the world cannot bridge the distance between us and the stars, and so God has to lift us the third time, and this time from earth into heaven.

Here are the three gifts of God to man: " Pardon and holiness and heaven." Growth in grace is commanded and expected in each state—growth for awhile in regeneration, growth for a lifetime in sanctification, and growth forever in heaven.

The second word is: " Go."

Paul uses it in Hebrews vi. 1: " Let us go on unto perfection."

The perfection here mentioned does not mean that absolute perfection that men at once think of when they hear the word. It does not mean deliverance from mistakes and blunders. Nor does it mean perfect knowledge. That we will never have, even in heaven. A minister, lately writing against holiness, remarked that when Paul said, " as many of us as be perfect," he referred to perfectness of knowledge. This the reader will feel at once is a mistake. We will be adding to our knowledge forever. The one perfection that the Bible speaks of is " perfect love." The taking out of the unfriendly element or nature, inbred sin, secures this blessed condition. O how the writer rejoices that it is our privilege to possess this perfection of love, with its invariable concomitants, purity, peace, and joy!

It is to this that Paul says: " Let us go on unto." He did not say, " Let us grow to it;" but " Let us go to it." Everybody ought to know that we grow in one direction, and go in another. Growth is vertical; to go is a horizontal movement. They are never the same. We grow in grace, but we go on to another blessing God has waiting for us. It is a blessing and experience that has a locality and boundary lines.

Dr. Clarke says that a true rendering of the passage is: "Let us be borne on immediately into perfection."

Be this as it may, growth in grace is a process, while to go on to perfect love is a performance. The first takes place insensibly; the second, in full consciousness of a great and gracious event. The first is gradual, running through the sweep of years; the other is momentary. The first never ceases, but goes on forever; while the other happens but once, and remains as an unchangeable blessing.

The Devil; the "Old Man."

These names have been confounded and actually made synonymous by a number of people.

As stated in a preceding chapter, the devil is no man at all, but was once an angel in heaven; and angels are a different order of beings from human beings.

The devil is a fallen archangel; the "old man" is a fallen human nature. It is a bias or tendency to sin, planted in our race through the work of the devil. The devil is the father of the "old man;" the "old man" is the only begotten child of the devil.

The sinner has both the devil and the "old man" in him; the regenerated soul has only the "old man;" the sanctified man has neither. With him the devil is on the outside, the "old man" is dead, and the New Man reigns in the heart without a rival.

Regeneration casts out the devil, and he should stay out; sanctification destroys the "old man," and he should stay dead.

The Bible never says, "Resist the 'old man,'" or "Put off the devil;" but just the other way, "Resist the devil," and "Put off the 'old man.'" We cannot escape from the presence of Satan, but can from inbred sin.

That Satan, however, can resow his tares in a sanctified heart, both the Bible and life teach. If he could get into the pure heart of Adam in Eden, he can certainly obtain entrance into sanctified souls that are not watchful and obedient, and fail to keep under "the blood." Then is it that the archenemy, taking unto himself seven other spirits, returns unto the house that had been swept and garnished after his ejection, and the last state of that man is worse than the first.

He who planted depravity in the heart of a pure man in the garden of Eden can sow it again in America in the soul of one who has been sanctified. The devil is not dead, though his children and species are slain all around him.

Alas that the garnished house can be devil-possessed again! Alas that the owner of the field of wheat should fall asleep, and the adversary, while he sleeps, should sow the tares of carnality once more! What a pity that, after having been delivered from an inheritance of evil, one would allow Satan to work directly in him, and reimpose what he had been graciously delivered from.

Regeneration cast out the hideous father; sanctification destroys the ugly son. May we live so that the devil will not reënter the soul and propagate his species, called the " old man."

SANCTIFICATION; ENTIRE SANCTIFICATION.

It is true that holiness people make these two terms synonymous in their conversations, but do not in their mind. In the first part of this chapter we used simply the word " sanctification," over against " consecration," but this was for convenience and brevity's sake. The Scripture recognizes a partial, and also a complete or entire sanctification. Just as the Bible tells of a state of love, and anoth-

er of perfect love; of blessing, and " the fullness
of the blessing;" so does it teach that we can be
sanctified in part, and again that we can be sanctified wholly.

This does not argue any imperfection or incom-
pleteness upon the part of God, but it is rather a
mark or indication of the progress or extent of his
work. It must never be forgotten that the work
of entire sanctification is an advanced movement,
an appearance and victory upon a new field, a
dealing with a different thing, and is not a repetition or going over of a former work.

Some people would degrade the blessing of holiness or entire sanctification into a mere reclamation. Reclamation from a backslidden state might
itself be called a repetition of divine work; God
doing his work over. But holiness, or entire sanctification, is God's destruction of inbred sin, and
his entrance into the heart as a perpetual indweller. This constitutes a distinct and different work,
and so cannot be called reclamation, or a repeated
work.

A recognition of this fact of partial and entire
sanctification would clear up difficulties in the
minds of many people, and put an end to countless paper and book controversies.

It is in recognition of this truth that Paul writes
to the Corinthians, calling them " sanctified," and
yet immediately afterwards speaks of their carnality; and while he calls them "new creatures" in
Christ Jesus, he bids them to " cleanse themselves
from all filthiness of the flesh and spirit, perfecting
holiness." The word "perfecting" means also
accomplishing.

He also writes to the Thessalonians, whose faith
had been spoken of abroad, and who were exam-
ples to all who believed in Macedonia and Achaia.
He prays for them thus: "And the very God of
peace sanctify you *wholly*."

The first fact of these Christians being called
sanctified the opponents of holiness notice; but
utterly neglect to mention the second fact of their
not being wholly sanctified, and thus fail to draw
the inevitable teaching and truth from the two facts
put together. And so they say to us: " Why do
you exhort us to be sanctified? All Christians are
sanctified! Does not Paul in his Epistles write to
the churches that they are sanctified?" Our reply is, Yes; but he does not call them wholly
sanctified; on the contrary, he exhorts them to
come on to this last-named blessing.

Regeneration is sanctification, but it is partial

sanctification; not an imperfect sanctification, but partial in the sense of something still remaining in the soul that it is not in the province and power of regeneration to touch or remove. In the erection of a house there are two classes of workers. They have different tools and labor on different things. When the carpenter, painter, and bricklayer have ended their work, it is noticed that, while their job is complete, yet the house itself is not finished. After them come the glazier, upholsterer, and plumber. One class worked at one thing; the other, at something totally distinct and different. Each work was perfect in itself, but the house was not complete or perfect until both works had been done.

So, to perfect the spiritual house in which God will dwell, two works are needed. Both works are perfect in themselves, but they are directed at two different states of the soul, and effect two different results or conditions. The first is aimed at personal sin and guilt; the second, at inherited or inbred sin. The first result is partial sanctification; the second is entire sanctification. Not until inbred sin is taken out of one by the baptism of the Holy Ghost and of fire, and not until Christ enters the soul as a perpetual indweller at the same time, is the grace and blessing of entire sanctification realized. This scriptural truth is strangely confirmed in the Church to-day by the two different experiences of regenerated and sanctified people.

A BAPTISM; THE BAPTISM.

Here are two words that are just the same, but preceded by two smaller words that make them widely dissimilar in their meaning. Short and simple as are these preceding words, multitudes in the Church of Christ have not as yet distinguished between them, and until they do they will never enter into the most gracious blood-bought privilege and experience of the Christian life.

"*A* baptism" of the Holy Spirit is any sweet, powerful, uplifting blessing that a child of God receives during his religious life. They come in time of trouble, after great temptation, and also after prolonged seasons of prayer. There are many of these baptisms coming all along the Christian life. They cannot be numbered without difficulty. They ought to be so many that one could not count them. These are the gracious refreshings and renewals that the opposers of sanctification refer to when they say, in derision of our claiming the second blessing, that they have received a hundred or a thousand blessings. Such speeches show that, while they know what "a baptism" is, they do not understand what is meant by the term "the baptism."

"*The* baptism" should come only once in the lifetime. Just as there is one regeneration, so should there be one sanctification or baptism of the Holy Ghost. In this sense there is "one baptism."

"A baptism" of the Holy Ghost passes away in its effects upon the heart; "the baptism" remains as a permanent gift and an abiding influence and power.

It was in reference to "the baptism" that Christ spoke when he directed his disciples to tarry at Jerusalem until they were endued with power. A few days before they had received "a baptism," when he breathed upon them and said, "Receive ye the Holy Ghost;" but "the baptism" came for the first time to them on the day of Pentecost.

It was in regard to this grace or blessing that Paul asked the disciples at Ephesus if they had "received the Holy Ghost" since they had believed. And it is a pertinent and proper question still. It should be urged on every Christian.

Not "Have ye received *a* baptism of the Spirit?"
To this question each one should be able to answer: "Yes, thousands of times." But here is the question: "Have ye received *the* baptism of the Holy Ghost?"

CHAPTER XXI.

WE all know that Christ brings salvation to the world; that men in the Old Testament dispensation were saved by faith in a Christ to come, as they are in the present dispensation saved by faith in a Christ who has come. A prospective faith once, a retrospective faith now, brings pardon to the sinner. Christ has always been the Door of Salvation; the Light, the Truth, the Way of Life to the nations of the world.

But in addition to this and other blessings of the atonement, there is to be recognized running through prophecy allusions to some gracious work the Saviour was to do for his Church and people. In lofty imagery and plain statement the prophets said that he would do certain things for the world, but a special thing for Zion or the Church. More than one agreed that this was to be his distinguishing mark or sign. We were to know him by this special and peculiar work.

It is significant that Zechariah bids Jerusalem rejoice, for "behold, thy King cometh unto *thee*."

Malachi declares the same fact, that the Messiah's first coming and movement should be in his *temple;* that his work would be like refiner's fire, that he would sit as a purifier of silver, and that his work should be wrought upon the *sons of Levi,* his own servants and people.

In Isaiah lxi. 3 this gracious work to be done in *Zion* (not the world) appears again. "To appoint unto them that mourn *in Zion,* to give unto them beauty for ashes, the oil of joy for mourning, the garment of praise for the spirit of heaviness."

Next is the testimony of the angel Gabriel. It is remarkable that when he announced to Mary the coming birth of the Messiah he passed over the other works of Christ, and mentioned this one to the wondering virgin: "Thou shalt call his name Jesus: for he shall *save his people from their sins.*"

Let the reader mark the passage. The author read it for years before he saw the precious truth that glittered like a gem down in the plain, familiar statement. The word is not that he will save sinners, but " *his people* from their sins."

After this is heard the voice of John the Baptist witnessing to the same truth in the words that the

Saviour had come to " thoroughly *purge his floor*,"
and again, " He shall baptize you with the Holy
Ghost and with fire."

Paul speaks of it in the words: " Christ also
loved the *church*, and gave himself for it; that he
might *sanctify* and cleanse it with the washing of
water by the word, that he might present it to
himself a glorious church, not having spot, or
wrinkle, or any such thing; but that it should be
holy and without blemish." The Revised Version
puts it: " That he might sanctify it, having cleansed
it," etc. So the second work is made clear, and
it is, as stated everywhere in the Scriptures, in
and upon the Church.

The Saviour himself repeatedly spoke of it, and
prepared his disciples for it. Luke says that he
" commanded them that they should not depart
from Jerusalem, but wait for the promise of the
Father, which, saith he, *ye have heard of me*."
It was so important that he had often spoken of
the coming blessing to them.

In the next verse he said to *his disciples:* " Ye
shall be baptized with the Holy Ghost not many
days hence." At another time during the forty
days of the resurrection life he said: " Behold, I
send the promise of my Father upon you: but tarry

16

ye in the city of Jerusalem, until ye be endued with power from on high."

What was this work or blessing?

Not pardon or regeneration, for the Church had known this experience all along. Abraham, Jacob, David, and countless multitudes were called God's children. "These all died in the faith," says Paul. Besides this the promise here of a peculiar work, grace, or blessing is made *to the Church*.

If after these prophesies, the utterances of the Saviour, and the emphatic statement of John the Baptist that the Messiah had a baptism of fire for his people; if after all this, when it finally came, as it did come on Pentecost, and proved to be only regeneration, the whole body of disciples would have been disappointed, the prophets could be shown to have uttered foolish and false statements, and the Baptist shown to be guilty of deceiving his hearers.

Suppose a father promised his children an unusually excellent morning meal, and when the hour arrived and all sat down full of expectancy they discovered before them the same old breakfast! What a mockery it would have been to the people, after all the glowing promises of John about a baptism of fire that they were to receive at the hands of the Saviour, when it was at last realized, to find that it was nothing more than what they had experienced before.

It is folly to call this blessing that we are speaking of regeneration, as some do in order to deny and get rid of a second work. There are overwhelming reasons why it is not possible to call it regeneration.

One is that this peculiar work of Christ is called a *baptism*, while regeneration we all understand is a birth. In addition to this we know that a birth and baptism are not only different things, but cannot take place at the same moment. The child is born, and, subsequently, baptized. So God's child is born first, and baptized with the Holy Ghost afterwards.

Secondly, Christ calls it an enduement of power, while regeneration is an impartation of life.

Thirdly, it is likened to " fire," and fire is never used as a symbol of regeneration. Water is the type of regeneration, and fire stands for holiness. "Our God is a consuming fire;" and when he sanctified his tabernacle and altar he did it with fire, and when he sanctified his disciples he did it with holy fire.

A fourth reason for knowing that this " baptism

of fire " was not regeneration is evidenced from
the fact that it fell upon believers.

Again, this promised work of the Messiah was
not a recovery from backsliding.

This would belittle the prophecy. Moreover,
the terms will not allow such an interpretation.
The disciples were not backsliders when they received this blessing. It is true that they had for-
saken Christ and fled, the night of his arrest, but
all had been forgiven and restored, even doubting
Thomas. Peter had been recommissioned on the
banks of Galilee, and Christ had breathed the
Holy Ghost upon them prior to his ascension and
the descent of this blessing.

Nor was this work of Christ to be a simple effu-
sion or outpouring of the Spirit in a transitory way.

It stands to reason that the prophets would not
uplift their voices for ages about a distinguishing
blessing that meant only a cupful of happiness for an
hour or a day to the individual when it came. Reason and Scripture both alike forbid such a thought.

Nor was it simply an anointing for work of the
apostles alone. Instead of the twelve receiving,
we read that it came upon one hundred and twenty disciples, composed not only of men, but of
women.

Nor was it a work to end on the morning of Pentecost, and with the one hundred and twenty.

Peter, standing up and addressing the wondering inhabitants of Jerusalem and strangers from every nation, said: "The promise is unto you, and to your children, and to all that are afar off, even as many as the Lord our God shall call."

Moreover, it could not and cannot as a work be regarded as simply a greater measure of the Spirit given to the child of God.

It is this and more. Peter forever settles that question in Acts xv. 8, 9, where, in identifying what had been done to Cornelius with what had happened to the disciples on Pentecost, he said that in the baptism of the Holy Ghost their hearts were *purified.* He put no difference, he says, between us and them, "purifying their hearts by faith." These words prove several things: first, that regeneration is not purity; secondly, that purity does not come by growth or development; and, thirdly, that there is another work of grace in the heart subsequent to regeneration.

Let the reader consider these facts, and then turn to the Scripture statements, "He shall come to his temple," "shall purify the sons of Levi," "shall save his people from their sins," "shall purge his floor," "shall baptize with the Holy Ghost and with fire;" and he is compelled to say that here is a great uplifting, purifying blessing to come upon the Church, and it is to come as the personal work of the Son of God. If the promise had never been fulfilled, the fact remains as taught by these and other words of prophecy that another grace or blessing distinct from pardon, different from regeneration, remains for the people of God.

Thousands in the centuries that have gone by have discovered the blessing through a humble, attentive study of the Bible. It exists for the child of God, whether he ever obtains it or not.

But some one will ask: "When was this blessing received by any one in the Bible?"

The reply is: First at Pentecost. What was the wonderful occurrence in the upper room but the first glorious and general fulfillment of the long-prophesied work and blessing of the Messiah. The long-promised, long-expected second blessing or work of grace had come at last. It came as narrated in the book of Acts four distinct times, and, thank God, has been coming ever since, and will continue to come with increasing frequency to the end of the world.

It fell first in Jerusalem, next in Samaria, the

third time in Cæsarea, and the fourth in Ephesus. First, on the Jews; secondly, on the Samaritans; thirdly, on the Romans; and fourthly, on the Greeks. All this being in perfect harmony with the words of Peter, "The promise is unto you, and to your children, and unto all that are afar off."

The first time it came upon the disciples in Jerusalem. It was obtained by a congregation of believers, of whom Christ had said they were " not of the world," were " branches of the true vine," and their " names were in the Book of Life; " and it came after they had been seeking, praying, and waiting for it ten days. The second chapter of Acts gives a full account of the blessed occurrence.

The second time it fell upon believers in Samaria who had been converted under the preaching of Philip. No unprejudiced mind can read the account of the revival held by Philip in Samaria when the people " received the word of God," " believed," and were " baptized," and there was " great joy in that city," without seeing that the subsequent blessing of the baptism of the Holy Ghost, which fell upon them under the teaching of Peter and John, came upon converted men and women.

The third time it came upon a *devout man* and his believing household in Cæsarea.

To escape the plain teaching of the second work of grace in the tenth chapter of Acts a number have set themselves to believe that Cornelius was a heathen sinner needing conversion, and received that blessing under the preaching of Peter.

But God's description of the centurion was that he was " a *devout man*, and one that *feared God* with all his house, which gave much alms to the people, and *prayed to God always*." The Book also says that these prayers and alms had been accepted of God; that he was of " good report among all the nations;" that he practiced fasting and seems to have been so spiritual that the instant Peter met him he at once saw that he was a man " accepted of God."

Some have supposed that the difficulty with Cornelius was that he had never heard the gospel, but this is completely refuted in the thirty-sixth and thirty-seventh verses, where Peter, in speaking to the Roman captain, said: " The word which God sent unto the children of Israel, preaching peace by Jesus Christ, *that word, I say, ye know*."

Peter's mission to Cornelius was to declare the special work of Christ upon the believer—viz., the baptism of the Holy Ghost.   So the Word says: "While Peter yet spake these words, the Holy Ghost fell on all them which heard the Word. And they of the circumcision which believed were astonished, as many as came with Peter, because that on the Gentiles also was *poured out the gift of the Holy Ghost*.   For they heard them speak with tongues, and magnify God."

Here was not remission of sins received, but the forty-fifth verse says: "The gift of the Holy Ghost." In the next chapter Peter tells the disciples in Jerusalem that it was the same blessing that they themselves had obtained at Pentecost: "As I began to speak, the Holy Ghost fell on them, as on us at the beginning."   Here Peter identifies the blessing Cornelius received with what came upon them on the morning of Pentecost.   It was a blessing received by believers and disciples.

The fourth recorded time that " the baptism " fell was in Ephesus.

It came, as always, upon believers.   Twelve " disciples " and " believers " they were called. Paul asked them: " Have ye received the Holy Ghost since ye believed?"   Their remarkable answer, according to the King James translation, was: " We have not so much as heard whether there be any Holy Ghost.'' Commentators and other scholars have long ago seen that this is an incorrect translation. The Revised Version puts it properly: '' We did not so much as hear whether the Holy Ghost was *given*.''

The truthfulness of this last translation is seen from the fact that these men said that they were the disciples of John the Baptist; and if so, must have heard of the Holy Ghost, for the Baptist emphasized the fact to the people that while he baptized with water Christ would '' baptize with the Holy Ghost.'' So to be the followers of John, and to have received his baptism, was to have heard of the Holy Ghost. But they had not heard that ''*the Holy Ghost was given*.''

Christ had already commenced baptizing with the Holy Ghost in Jerusalem, Samaria, and Cæsarea, but this was far away in Asia Minor, and there were no telegraph wires and steam railways, and news traveled slowly. They had not heard that the Holy Ghost had been given or poured out.

Now let the reader say what it was that they immediately received under the instruction of Paul. If pardon, the verse should read '' then they received the remission of sins.'' Instead of that, the Scripture says: ''And when Paul had laid his hands upon them, *the Holy Ghost came on them;* and they spake with tongues, and prophesied." Just exactly what was seen at Pentecost, for it was the same blessing.

These facts show conclusively that the long-promised blessing to be brought by the Messiah to the Church is not regeneration that he gives to the repenting world, but something altogether different, inasmuch as it is for the Church, and is a work wrought in the hearts of believers. In a word, the God-man, the New Man, has come to destroy the " old man," and so impart to his people the blessing of sanctification or holiness.

Christ knew, and the Church is steadily finding out, through the ages, that time, Christian work, growth in grace, repression of sin, old age, and sorrow are all alike powerless to produce heart purity or holiness.

It is the blood of Jesus alone that can cleanse from all sin. It is his power alone that can destroy inbred sin and create clean hearts. And so he has come to his Church with this great blessing. He has a diadem of beauty for her head. He has beautiful garments of purity for her form. He has a blessing for her that will make her arise, shine, rejoice, and take the world for him. It is the distinguishing blessing of the Messiah. He comes *first* to his temple, though there be many houses in the world. He will " purify the sons of Levi," said Malachi. He will "save his people from their sins," said the angel. " He shall baptize you with the Holy Ghost and with fire," said John. " He will sanctify his Church," said Paul. And then what? Well, in the might, beauty, and glory of the second work, the Church will sweep out of Jerusalem over Judea, through Samaria unto the uttermost parts of the earth, carrying light, life, salvation, and holiness everywhere.

This is the second work of grace. Pardon and peace is the first; purity and power is the second. God for Christ's sake gives the former in salvation; but Christ brings the latter in the baptism of fire.

"*He* shall baptize you " (not the Holy Ghost), " *He* shall baptize you *with* the Holy Ghost and with fire." And lo! when it came upon the disciples, Peter explaining to the wondering Jews, cried out: " This Jesus . . . being by the righthand of God exalted, . . . hath shed forth this which ye now see and hear."

O that every Christian and Church would get ready for this blessed grace and work of the Son

of God which destroys the " old man," enthrones
the New Man, purifies and empowers the people
of God, and sends forth the Church singing, shouting, victorious, and irresistible to the conquest of
the world.

> O that it now from heaven might fall,
>   And all my sins consume!
> Come, Holy Ghost, for thee we call,
>   Spirit of burning, come.

CHAPTER XXII.

ONE cause is the lack of a clear, definite preaching on the subject. It is remarkable, when this doctrine is properly presented, what a flame of holy fire begins to burn at once in many hearts, and how many enter into the gracious experience. On the other hand, the work declines when the pulpit becomes silent. So it blazed in the time of Wesley and Asbury, who constantly pressed it, and so it declined for forty or fifty years because the preachers were silent; and so it swelled again and rolled on in the time of such men as Finney and Inskip, who enjoyed and urged it on the people. In a large Southern city two persons possessed the blessing of sanctification for twenty-five years or more, but they did not proclaim it, and the pulpits were silent at the same time, and there was not a single additional sanctification. But a few years ago a preacher conducted a revival meeting at that place, presented the doctrine, and some forty people at once swept into the blessing.

This remarkable revival or languishing of the

experience conditional upon the faithful preaching
and witnessing of God's servants is not to be used
as an argument against the strength or divinity of
the doctrine. The fact is that the same thing pre-
vails in regard to every doctrine. The knowledge
of justification by faith died out in the Church because not preached: and there are many doubters
to-day in regard to the doctrine of hell, because
we lack the tender, tearful, solemn, and awful
preaching that brings conviction.

Two facts have forcibly impressed us. One is
that a general kind of preaching on sanctification;
or when it is presented as a far-away attainment,
as being a vague, endlessly progressive work; that
such preaching never awakens opposition, never
seems to move the people, and never results in a
case of sanctification. The explanation of the last
fact is evident. What is the use of struggling for
a thing that is not to be obtained? A remarkable
proof of the truth of the second work is seen in the
fact that it invariably infuriates the devil, is opposed by worldly Church members, awakens a
great antagonism on one side and as great a hope
and pursuit on the other, and results in every case
in a number obtaining the blessing. The second
fact is that a preacher who has not the blessing of

sanctification may preach on the subject as often as he will, and two curious results will be observable. First, no one will become offended; and second, no one will obtain the blessed experience.

It is the confession of the experience that so arouses Satan. He is willing for people to declare the fact of the experience, if they will not say that they have it. This accounts for the first result in the above case. As for the second, the failure of the people to enter into the blessing under such preaching is accounted for by a fact that has always been manifest in the spiritual life, and that is that a man cannot lead or lift people higher in the divine life than he has gone himself. Let the reader look where he will, and at whom he will, and tell us what preacher who denies the doctrine of sanctification by faith can show us souls rejoicing in purity of heart and perfect love as the result of the preaching of gradual sanctification. While on the other hand there are hundreds of ministers in the land who " press the instantaneous blessing " (Wesley) who can point to two and three hundred witnesses every year.

A second cause with many for failing to recognize and realize the blessing of sanctification is that it does not agree with their theology.

This can hardly be said of Methodist theology; for Wesley, Clarke, Benson, Watson, Smith, Ralston, and others, clearly present the second work of grace. If the people would study these writers, this objection would fall. The misfortune is, however, that the people fail to go to the fountain heads of our theological system, and listen instead to those who quote them with a mind prejudiced against the holy doctrine. There is a great difference here!

The Methodist Church would be amazed to-day if she knew how few of her preachers have ever read Mr. Wesley's little volume on " Christian Perfection." Some have read a few pages, some have skimmed; but many have not read a line in it, and few ever read it through. And yet all feel qualified to say what Mr. Wesley thought and said on the subject. We have prominent laymen in our Church opposing holiness who never had in their hands this book of the founder of their Church. And yet it is a work that Mr. Wesley never recalled, nor retracted therefrom a single utterance.

We would add another fact: that we never yet met a Methodist preacher who had read Mr. Wesley's Journal through, and few who have read much of it, and yet it is in this Journal that he has

17

so much to say about the second work of grace. They all can quote from his letter to Maxwell, because so often printed in religious newspapers of to-day, and because it is a warning against extremism, but are not so familiar with the book itself from which it is taken, where Mr. Wesley writes of the wonderful work of grace going on among the people, and which he calls the second blessing, and declares to be the undoubted work of God.

This much we would say in regard to the theological objection, if there was one: That if we saw many people in an experience of the spiritual life that had lifted them far above their and our own former regenerated experience, and we saw that there were many passages in the Scripture that favored, described, and otherwise taught such a blessing, then we would believe in it, and seek it with the whole soul, whether our theology taught it or not. Theologies are of man. They are men's conceptions of Bible teachings or truths, and can never equal the Bible itself. As students go deeper into the Word, and the Spirit reveals, theologies grow. Hence it is that we have seen them carried to the anvil and sometimes to the dissecting table. Sometimes the theology of a denomination has to be brought to the legislative department of the Church, and there be enlarged to fit the body of the growing experience of the people of God. Thank God, the Methodist Church is under no need to do this! The second divine work, or holiness received by faith, is taught by her founder, her commentators, and leading theologians. There are other denominations not so fortunate. But of this we are confident: that in the near future the people of more than one Church will have their theological garments on the legislative tailoring table, with instructions to cut them after the pattern of full salvation, so as to fit the experience of the people. Between a blessed religious experience and a defective theology some denominations are called to decide. The author would advise them to hold on to their experience, and as soon as possible mend and perfect their theology.

A third cause of the failure of many to recognize and realize the blessing of heart purity is that they demand to understand all about it before obtaining the experience. They ask countless questions on the subject. It must agree not only theologically, but physiologically and psychologically, with their notions. It must be susceptible of mathematical proof, and not have a shadow of doubt

resting upon it.   They must be satisfied thoroughly
on every point that may be raised by reason or
doubt before they will even begin to seek for the
blessing.

Their attitude is precisely similar to that of
Nicodemus when he was asking Christ to explain
the mystery of regeneration.   It will be remembered that the Saviour did not explain, but likened
it to the incomprehensible coming and going of
the wind.   " Thou knowest not whence it cometh or whither it goeth."   If the Lord said this
of regeneration, what would he have stated about
this work which the Bible calls the " mystery of
the gospel" and the " secret of the Lord?"
The attitude of the questioners and doubters of
sanctification is also like that of the unbelieving
world toward Christianity.   Everything must be
explained to the skeptic before he will even entertain the idea of believing.   The trinity—the dual
nature of Christ—the character of the resurrection, and other gospel mysteries, must all be dem-
onstrated and proved with the clearness of an
arithmetical sum on the blackboard.   Then, perhaps, he will descend a few steps from the proud
throne of reason and consider the case as it re-
lates to him personally.   How our regenerated

brethren would smilingly say to the skeptic or unbeliever after this manner: "There are some things that reason cannot grasp, but God has given us the power to believe and accept where we cannot understand. It is not necessary to understand a thing in order to be blessed by it. A babe does not comprehend its mother. A man cannot unravel the mystery of the sun, and yet he is cheered and blessed by its beams. Even so believe in Christ, and thou shalt be saved." Thus do regenerated men talk to unbelievers, and yet straightway forget all their arguments when brought face to face with the mystery of sanctification.

If the writer had waited until he understood all the faith-and-reason-trying features of sanctification, he never would have obtained the blessing. Instead of this, he first secured the pearl of great price, determining to study its nature afterwards. He obtained the blessing first, knowing that he had all the present life and the life to come to explore the heights and depths of the gracious mystery. He has never been sorry that he pursued that plan.

There is one lesson that God's children have to learn over and over. They first mastered it at conversion, but they forgot it, and it has to be re-

learned many times.   This lesson is that obedience to God is the condition of spiritual knowledge.   It is not by reasoning that the world knows
God or the things of God.   The Bible says so,
and we all know it to be so.   "If any man will
do his will, he shall know of the doctrine."   Obedience to the Word of God inducted us into the
regenerated life; obedience brings us to know the
mind of Christ; obedience reveals duty; and obedience to certain divine requirements will bring a
man into the experience of sanctification.   Experience alone can clear up the darkness and mystery of the doctrine.   Regeneration was once dark;
but when the pardoning grace of God was felt,
how clear!   Sanctification seems to have heavy
clouds and shadows resting upon it; but once entered upon, the clouds are seen to skirt the edge
and border alone, while the life itself is a Beulah
Land of brightness and glory.

We cannot understand a road until we travel it.
It is absurd for one to try to picture its topography
—its peculiar features of bridge and woodland, cot-
tage home, village, church spire, and country field
until he has traveled along its length.   All description will fail of the reality.   Just as absurd is it
for a man to demand to understand sanctification

before he has entered upon the gracious and wonderful experience.

The way for a person to do is, first, to get it,
and then take his time to understand. When seeking pardon and regeneration we were not the least
concerned about where the doctrine stood in the
economy of salvation; what preceded and what
followed. A preacher was telling us at the time
about the force of the subjunctive mood in a certain verse of invitation. But what did we care
for this subjunctive mood? We were after pardon.
This was the mood that filled us! So a man who
is hungry for holiness, and panting for Christ and
his fullness, will not worry his head about the theological position of the doctrine of holiness, nor
about the effect of sanctification on his posterity,
nor about the new relation he sustains to God, nor
about his moral state in case of relapse. These
things do not occupy his mind. His one desire is
for purity, his one cry is, " My God, give me a
holy heart"—and he gets it!

The man involved in tenses and moods and
Greek roots, and who is worried about psychol-
ogy and theology, does not get it. That is just the
difference. The Jews did not analyze the manna;
they simply and sensibly gathered it, ate it, and

lived. They did not take a hammer, file, and acids and go to examining and analyzing the brazen serpent; they simply looked and were saved.

A fourth cause for the blindness of many in regard to this great blessing is, that they are not yearning for the experience. Let the reader run his eye mentally over the congregations he knows in the land. Who among them is panting for holiness and perfect Christlikeness "as the hart panteth after the water brook?" Preachers and religious journals alike all over the country are deploring the coldness, deadness, and worldliness of the Church. The people, as a rule, are satisfied with a low justified state. They want enough religion to save them from hell, but not an amount that would entail the sacrifice of certain practices and pursuits and the entire loss of the world. All of them have just as much religion as they want; if they desired more, they would have more. They are satisfied to live at a poor, dying rate.

The force of the cause mentioned above is now to be seen. Spiritual hunger and thirst not only precede being filled with righteousness, but they somehow clarify the moral vision and discover almost invariably the way of holiness. To be without this hunger and thirst is to be without the de-

sire for a higher experience and without the power
to see that there is such a blessing for the soul.
To all such the preaching of a holy heart as obtainable by consecration and faith is not only dis-
tasteful, but, sad to say, is absolute foolishness.

We mention a fifth cause why many of God's
people fail to come into the blessing. This reason
is found in the reproach connected with the doctrine and experience. It has always been attended
with reproach, and will be until the millennium.
Let the reader inquire into the secret of religious
persecution in the past, and he will find the doctrine of holiness always involved. The antagonism
and abuse of Mr. Wesley was not occasioned by
his views of justification, but by his preaching the
doctrine of Christian perfection. There is no
truth in Christianity that so arouses the fury of
devils and men as that of the destruction of the
" old man," or full salvation from sin.

If any child of God wants to know what reproach and suffering are in the Christian life, let
him obtain the experience of sanctification and
express it before the people. If a man gets it and
keeps quiet, all will go well except the blessing
itself. But if he presumes to testify and preach
the glorious truth that Christ can make the heart

pure, and declares at the same time that he has done this work for him, then look out for outside trouble at once. The hatred felt in various quarters toward this Christ-honoring and blood-exalting doctrine is as sorrowful a spectacle as it is amazing. It is unmistakable. It appears in the eye, is heard in the voice, is declared in the freezing manner, drips from the editorial pen, rings in the attack made upon it in ecclesiastical assemblies, and is read in Church appointments. Meantime the man himself is at first filled with surprise at the state of affairs. He is conscious that he never loved the Church and the brethren as fervently before, that his ministry was never more fruitful, that he never preached with greater spiritual power; and yet, behold! he finds reproach, reproach, reproach on all sides. He was made to groan by his Church until he obtained the blessing of perfect love, and now he is made to groan again because he has obtained it.

This fact of reproach decides the matter with many. They would like the blessing of sanctification, but not at such a cost. They would like to have a holy heart, but they want to have an easy time and be popular with everybody at the same time. A most impossible thing! And so many turn from this crowning blessing of Christianity. Some prefer to be some great man's little man than to be God's man. Some are unwilling to forfeit episcopal favor. Some are not ready to give up large city churches and " go out not knowing whither they go." Some are unwilling to jeopardize their chances for the episcopate. All are unwilling that reproach and ridicule should be fastened upon them, and that all manner of things should be said about them. The pearl of full salvation is too costly. They are not ready like the merchantman to pay down all their substance for it.

There is a blessed experience of coming to Christ, finding everything, living in his service while he looks on us and loves us; there is another and higher experience in which one sells out in the deepest sense of the word, leaves everything, and follows Christ. We are called to it by the Saviour. But many turn away sorrowful. They have great possessions — reputation, influence, earthly hopes and prospects, and other things that they are unwilling to sacrifice. Moses *chose* affliction—*preferred* the reproach of Christ—but they do not.

They fail to realize that the reproaches of Christ are greater riches than the treasures of Egypt or

the entire world. Such a life may look like a carcass, but it is a carcass full of honey. We may
appear like deluded or demented people to the
Michals laughing at us from the window; but the
ark of God is with us; we know we have the truth;
our own mouth is filled with holy laughter, our
heart with praises; and so we can stand with perfect resignation the amusement of an unbelieving
world.

Here, then, are some of the causes that prevent
Christians from having the "old man" slain, and
entering at once upon the enjoyment of full salvation: lack of definite preaching on the subject,
theological difficulties, the demand to understand
beforehand all mysteries connected with the doctrine, the absence of real yearning for the blessing, and the reproach that always attends the experience.

What a pity that any of these things should be
allowed to be a swinging sword of fire to keep the
soul out of an Eden filled with spiritual beauty,
and glorious with the unclouded and perpetual
presence of the Lord!

Reader, have you followed the writer through
the pages of this volume, and do you desire the
death of the "old man," and would you be clothed

upon with the New Man? Would you have sin to go, and holiness enter, and Christ reign without a rival continually in the heart? Then come at once to the Strong Man, the Mighty to save, the Wonderful, the Prince of Peace, the Saviour of the world. You will find him " outside the gate." " Wherefore Jesus also, that he might *sanctify* the people with his own blood, suffered without the gate. Let us *go* forth therefore unto him without the camp, bearing his reproach."

" Let us go." We have lost already too much time in waiting. Alas for the sad hours and days of spiritual failure that should not have been since the Deliverer has come !

" Unto him." It is Christ we want, not time nor death nor growth. We want the New Man who conquered Satan, and can slay the " old man."

" Without the camp." Some victims were slain in the temple court, and one was offered outside the gate. Thus the Bible teaches the double work and cure. The sanctifying blood is not believed on in the camp; alas that we have to go outside until to-dayto find it.

" Bearing his reproach." We cannot obtain the blessing apart from a certain ignominy. The nails, thorns, sponge of vinegar, mocking, and re-jection, all await us who would come to the puri-fying blood outside the gate.

Nevertheless, let us go to him. We will never be sorry. With the " old man " dead, and the New Man reigning within us, how can one be sorry? Nor is this all; for in the tenth verse of the thirteenth chapter of Hebrews we read that we will " have an altar, whereof they have no right to eat which serve the tabernacle." Pro-moted from Levites to priests, there is a different and richer fare according to the word just quoted. The table is set, and we eat in the presence of our enemies, our heads are anointed with oil, our cups run over, goodness and mercy follow us all the days of our lives, and we shall dwell in the house of the Lord forever.

THE END.

Made in United States
Troutdale, OR
08/21/2023

12271644R00170

AND WHEN I FALL ASLEEP

THE OBJECTS IN MY HOUSE

MOVE SLOWLY TO MY SIDE

AND WHISPER SECRET NAMES

THE NAMES THEY USUALLY HIDE

AND WHEN I FALL AWAKE

I TRY TO WRITE THEM DOWN

BUT REAL NAMES ARE LIKE SAND

THEY SPILL OUT OF MY HANDS

LOCATION Winchelsea Beach

D U S T C O V E R S

DUST COVERS : THE COLLECTED SANDMAN COVERS 1989-1997.

Originally published in single magazine form as THE SANDMAN 1-75, THE
SANDMAN SPECIAL #1, THE VERTIGO GALLERY: DREAMS &
NIGHTMARES No. 1, THE SANDMAN GALLERY No. 1, and THE ENDLESS
GALLERY No. 1, in the SkyBox Vertigo Trading Cards and The SANDMAN
collections PRELUDES & NOCTURNES, THE DOLL'S HOUSE, DREAM
COUNTRY, SEASONS OF MISTS, A GAME OF YOU, FABLES &
REFLECTIONS, BRIEF LIVES, WORLDS' END, THE KINDLY ONES and
THE WAKE.

Published by Watson-Guptill Publications, a division of BPI Communications, Inc.,
1515 Broadway, New York, NY 10036 under license from DC Comics,
a division of Warner Bros.-A Time Warner Entertainment Company,
1700 Broadway, NY 10019.

Cover, introduction and compilation copyright © 1997 DC Comics.

Printed in Canada

10 9 8 7 6 5 4 3 2

2 3 4 5 6 7 8 9 /06 05 03 02 01 00

Cover and Publication design by Dave Mckean @ Hourglass.

GEA'SADH/FLOWING CD cover (page 196) is © 1991 Virgin/Venture
Productions and is reprinted with the permission of Virgin Records Limited.

LUMEN CD cover (page 197) is © 1995 Virgin/Venture Productions
and is reprinted with the permission of Virgin Records Limited.

Artwork by Dave McKean Page 199 © 1993 The All Blacks B.V.

From the Roadrunner Records album cover "Dreams of the Carrion Kind"

by DISINCARNATE. All Rights Reserved. Used by permission.

All photos by Dave McKean and used by permission unless otherwise noted.

The lyrics on pages 1, 208 and the hardback case cover are from the song

"Mixed Metaphors" and are © 1997 Dave McKean, reprinted by permission.

The stories, characters, and incidents featured in this publication are entirely fictional.

Cataloging -In-Publication Data is available from the Library of Congress

ISBN: 0-8230-4632-X (pbk)

For DC Comics:

1997

DUST COVERS

The Collected Sandman covers 1989-1996

[L O C A T I O N] Drawing Board

by Dave McKean

With a new story and commentary
by Neil Gaiman and Dave McKean.

Sandman characters created by Gaiman, Kieth and Dringenberg

Page numbers start with page 4

The Last Sandman story.

[This was Neil's introductory paragraph to me, which I thought appropriate to print here. We are, after all, behind the scenes.] **D M**

Which may or may not be true, but is a wonderful thing to type at the top of a sheet of paper. Or at the top of a screen, to be more accurate.

So I'm sitting at the bottom of the garden in my gazebo in the snow, being harassed by a small orange cat who quacks and keeps trying to show me how much he loves me by rubbing his face on mine and sitting on the keyboard, and sooner or later I shall throw him out. I don't mind him sitting on my head: It's the trying to type I object to.

We've discussed this story a little over the years. (Sorry about that. Brief interruption, due to taking small orange cat and flinging him through the air into a snowdrift. Small orange cat thought this was great sport and is waiting by the door to try to persuade me to let him in and do it again.) And these were the things we decided we wanted in this story:

1) More prose than comics - one or two illustrations to a page.

2) Something that had the kind of look that was of a piece with the covers.

3) Something about the original 'Sandman story.'

I want to write something anecdotal - something that is obviously a sort of personal coda to SANDMAN, rather than something that extends any part of the story...

NG

I promised I would never forget my childhood.
I promised myself I would never forget. It was the books that did it, the sour, silly tales of children who were not children, which I read, as a boy, and knew that the author must have forgotten. I hold on to my childhood now, like a charm.

When I was two, or three, I asked my mother where the grit came from, in the corners of my eyes, in the morning, when I woke.
I was an odd, precocious child:
I would dictate poetry to her, and she would write it down.
She said, "He comes to you.
In the night. The Sandman.
He sprinkles sand in your eyes, so you sleep.
And then you dream.
He has a bag of sand. A sack of sand.
That is the sand you find in your eyes when you wake."

Now, understand, I was a child who believed all he was told. My parents told me true things.

Our car was stolen once, and Churchill died. I knew this, because they told me. I looked out of the window, when the snow was on the ground, and saw an animal sliding through the snow, and learned from them that it was a stoat (in its winter coat, an ermine).

My parents taught me my wooden letters. I painted the consonants blue, with paint, the vowels in red, with nail lacquer. Even today red nail polish smells to me like vowels.

So I believed in the Sandman, when I was three. Ask me if I still do...

Alan Moore encountered John Constantine in a restaurant in South London, after he had been writing him for several years. They did not talk. I dreamed once of Morpheus. I knew what it felt like to be him, to look out of his eyes. (Which are not eyes. That was the strangest part of it. They were not eyes at all.)
When Holly, my oldest daughter, was four or five she would come to me at night, complaining she could not sleep, and I would tell her of the Sandman, and his pouch of magic sand, which would send her to dreamland.
I told her I had some of that sand. Only a pinch, but it was enough.
I would blow imaginary sand into her eyes, and she would smile, satisfied.
Then she would return to her bed, and sleep easily, and I would return to writing.
I wrote all the night, in those days. Every word was written in the dark.
I have never encountered Morpheus in reality, have had no encounters with the Sandman, except, perhaps, for one, which I will come to in time.

Death is another matter. She follows us around. The original drawing came from Mike Dringenberg. I showed it to Dave McKean on a Thursday evening in Chelsea. Afterwards, we went to the My Old Dutch Pancake House, where we would go and eat pancakes and talk about art.

That night, our waitress wore black. She had long black hair, and a silver ankh, and a perfect, almost elfin face. We stared after her, and discussed showing her the drawing, but embarrassment conquered all, and we did not.

Even so, I took it as an omen. I knew her, now.

Dave saw her once on a plane to San Diego. It was a most unpleasant journey: a passenger on the plane from London had a fatal heart attack, forcing the plane to land while the body was removed. The living passengers were forbidden to get off. "And there was one of your fans on the plane," said Dave, when he told me about it, several weeks later. "Yeah?"
"One of those girls in black, with an ankh," he said. Dave is a very practical person, and not given to odd fancies, such as believing in people he knows perfectly well that I made up.

There have been times, though, only a few, when reality frayed and thinned. Half a decade ago I was in New York, on Hallowe'en. I was in the Village, with some friends, watching the parade. *Batman Returns* had just come out, and the parade was crawling with fetishistic Batmen and Catwomen. I'd just finished writing *The Doll's House*.

In the crowds I became separated from the people I was with.

He walked away, and a few moments later I
ran into my friends. They thought I was a bit subdued, and I was.
We went to a diner called *Lox Around the Clock*, and our waitress looked very familiar.
Me: You look like Death.
Death/waitress: You mean I look like Hell. These Hallowe'en crowds, huh?
Me: No, I... never mind.

And I wondered, even then, with all the people in Sandman, why I should encounter a minor
demon I was not even interested in, instead of any of the other characters.
I dismissed the incidents as a waking dream, a fantasy, a peculiarly vivid moment of what if.
And perhaps that was all it was.
I wrote Choronzon into *Season of Mists*, though. It seemed the least I could do.

One last memory, on this perfect day. The eagles are soaring the updrafts, above the woods, and in my head I am soaring with them.
It was in England. Holly was five or six, and she had one of the illnesses of childhood.
My wife had gone to bed, exhausted from caring for the little girl.

I was working, through the night. When Holly would cry, I would go in to her, and wipe the sticky sweat from her forehead with a damp face-flannel, and give her a little water to sip. She felt like she was burning up. I took her temperature, and carried her into the bathroom, and rubbed her back while she threw up, and put her back to bed. And I worried.
She would cry to me, and sob, but the words she cried made no sense.

And when she settled back to her restless sleep, I would walk to my study, and sit in front of the computer, and write.

And then she would begin to sob once more, and would walk back down the little corridor, to see if there was something I could do.

It was gone 3:00am, and I was fighting a deadline. I tried to ignore her cries, and to write. Then she stopped crying, and began, loudly, to scream, and I ran down the corridor to her bedroom.

There was a man standing over her, dressed in black, his hands and face moon-white, and he was sprinkling sand on her face.

That was what I saw.

I started to say something, but as I opened my mouth, I saw what I was seeing.

The face was the moon, seen through the trees. The hand, only a branch of a beech tree, bathed in moonlight. The cloak was the reflection of the room, in the window-glass. A moment of optical illusion, that was all.

But my daughter was, finally, sleeping peacefully, and when I touched her forehead, her skin was no longer on fire.
I left her to sleep, and, exhausted, turned out the lights and went to bed myself.

I remember that moment, and the Hallowe'en fantasy, and the various encounters with Death-girls, as something special, set aside from the rest of Sandman. But then, the writing of Sandman was, in itself, a tangled strand of coincidences.

Ask me by daylight if I believe in Morpheus, or any of the other characters I invented and I'll smile at you, and tell you how hard it is to believe in people when you know they came out of your head.

Ask me late at night, though, whisper it to me as my head touches the pillow in the moment before I sleep...

I do not know what answer you will get.

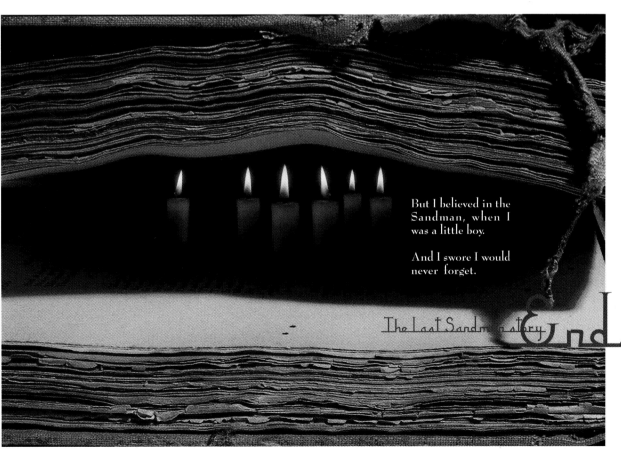

But I believed in the Sandman, when I was a little boy.

And I swore I would never forget.

The Last Sandman story ᴇnds

I remember driving through London in 1989 with Neil and saying that I wanted to make a cover with a wooden frame around it, take it outside and set fire to it. I remember this as the key to the Sandman covers for some reason. This was not going to be a comic series about a specific character who looks a specific way. It was about a concept, the idea of dreaming. The covers should in their own way take the preconceptions of how a comic cover looks out into the garden and set fire to them.

Did we ever get that radical? No, of course not. But several sacred cows were sacrificed along the way. Several experiments tried. Some succeeded, others failed. Several times I found what I felt to be a personal voice through these covers, only to bin that idea and start from scratch next time.

Some ground was covered, if measured only by the rather timid burning of number 4, compared to the petrol-doused number 69. The notion that the Sandman had to be on each cover was the first to go. At the top of each issue would be the word "Sandman" so we all thought this was sufficient clue as to which comic readers would be looking at.

The first eight covers were a portrait gallery. **D M**

Preludes & Nocturnes collection hardback front cover

1995

Clay, photography, Mac

1949 x 1654 pixels

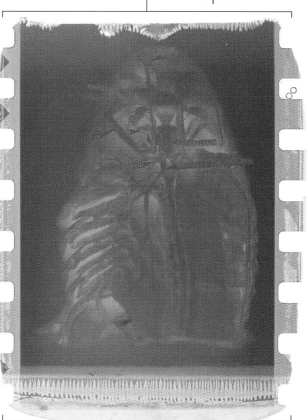

Personal photograph

1997

Photography

35mm negative

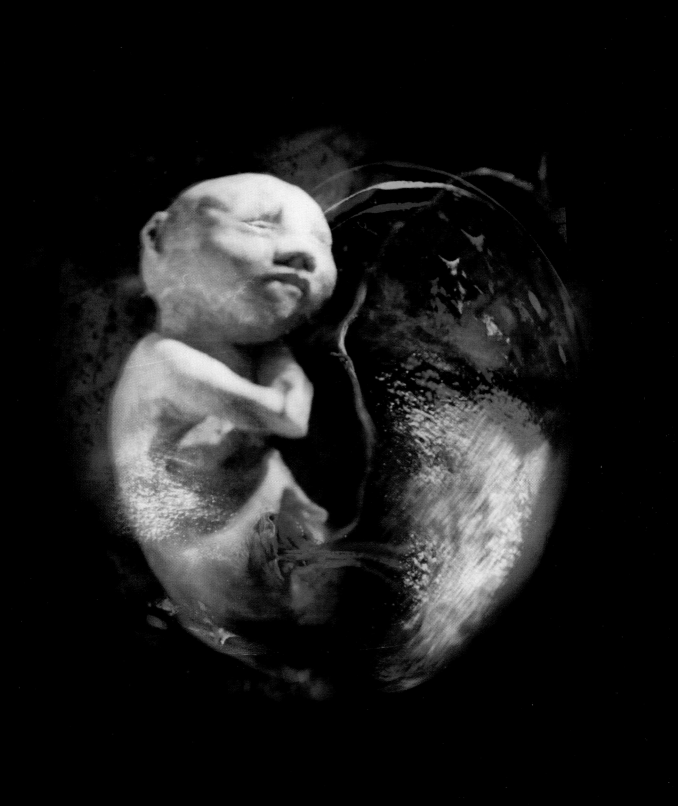

1. The first SANDMAN cover was the most exciting. Dave suggested the shelves down the side (something that I vaguely remember was inspired by the film poster for Peter Greenaway's **The Belly of An Architect**), and together we scoured Covent Garden, looking for things to put on the shelves — that was where Dave found the Hourglass and the Buddha and the black cat. The book **The Gates of Dawn** was published by Mills and Boon, famed across the British Empire for their romance books, and Dave carefully obliterated their names from the spine, in case people thought SANDMAN might be a romance.

The Sandman image on the cover was inspired by Peter Murphy, the ex-Bauhaus singer and Maxell tape model, because when artist Mike Dringenberg saw the original sketches for the character he said "He looks just like Peter Murphy"; and we were relieved that he looked like someone. The first eight covers were conceived as a portrait gallery.

NG

The Sandman no. 1 cover

1989

Acrylic, graphite, oil pastel, wooden frame, various objects

24 x 36 inches

Preludes & Nocturnes collection paperback cover

1991

Acrylic, ink, oil pastel, wooden type tray, painted eggs, tissue, driftwood

22 x 12 inches

2. The things in the jars which look like internal organs were actually made of plasticene. After a while they dissolved and turned into sludge. **NG**

The Sandman no. 2 cover

1989

Acrylic, oil pastel, wooden frame, filled jars

24 x 36 inches

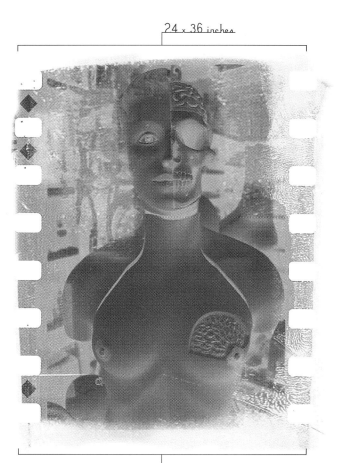

Personal photograph

1997

Photographic negative

35mm

Die gotische Schrift war urspru
stabenschrift · Deshalb heißt d

3. Dave's first work for DC had been doing the covers for HELLBLAZER. In this he had been aided, as a model, by his friend Neil Jones, who looked a bit like John Constantine, only not as seedy, and owned his own trench coat. This was Neil's first appearance on a SANDMAN cover. **N G**

The Sandman no. 3 cover

1989

Acrylic, graphite, ink, wooden frame, paper collage, cigarette package

24 x 36 inches

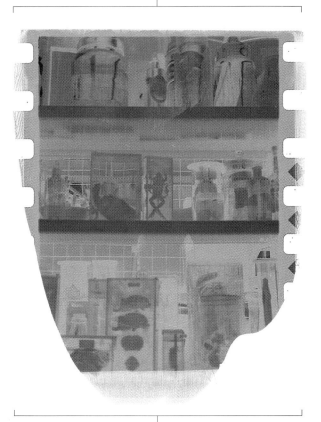

Personal photograph

1997

Photographic negative

35mm

"Genius . . . is the transcendent capacity
for taking trouble, first of all."
— THOMAS CARLYLE

4. Lucifer. The very young David Bowie, back when he was still a folkie, was our inspiration for Lucifer. This cover reappears as part of the cover of SANDMAN no. 23. The observant will notice a few small burnt bits which we did in lieu of setting it alight and photographing it while it burned. **NG**

The Sandman no. 4 cover

1989

Acrylic, ink, oil pastels, wooden frame, paper collage, fire damage

24 x 36 inches

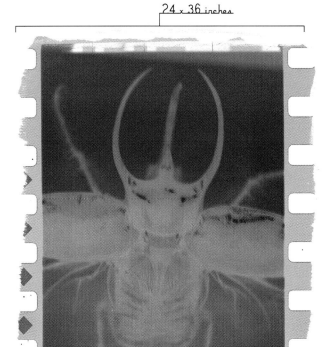

Personal photograph

1997

Photographic negative

35mm

5. Probably the nearest Dave has ever got — or will ever get — to Jack Kirby was this picture of the very young Scott Free. I like the chains and padlocks, which give you an idea of how large these covers were. **NG**

The Sandman no. 5 cover

1989

Acrylic, ink, oil pastels, wooden frame, wire mesh, chains, components

24 x 36 inches

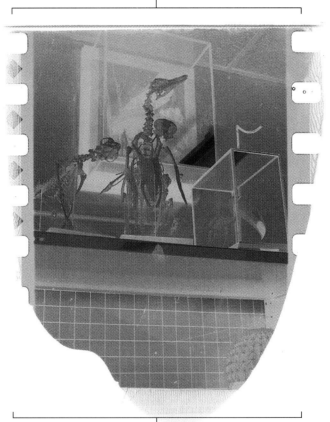

Personal photograph

1997

Photographic negative

35mm

6. At this point we began the headlong slide into obscurantism that served us so well. This is Dr. Dee, I think. Or at least, it's his eye. My favorite bit of this cover is the face formed by the broken coffee cup. **NG**

The Sandman no. 6 cover

1989

Acrylic, ink, oil pastels, wooden frame, various objects

24 x 36 inches

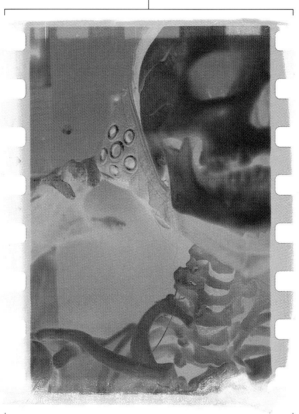

Personal photograph

1997

Photographic negative

35mm

7. If you look very carefully you

can see the cover to SANDMAN

no. 1 is painted on the fabric in
                    [Actually it's a xerox laid underneath
the middle of this cover. Once you
                    coarse muslin, so it just shows through
have seen it you will never again be
                    the holes in the material. **D M**]
able to un-see it. **N G**

The Sandman no. 7 cover

1989

Acrylic, ink, oil pastels, hesian, wooden frame, photography, door knob

24 x 36 inches

Personal photograph

1997

Photographic negative

35mm

8. I would phone Dave up and talk to him about the covers. Sometimes I'd want something specific. We talked about Death quite a bit. Dave saw the original sketch of her that Mike Dringenberg did, and was unsurprised when our waitress that evening (at the "My Old Dutch" Pancake house in the King's Road, Chelsea) was the spitting image of the character Mike had designed, ankh and all.

I phoned him up and talked to him about this cover. He described it to me. A few days later I phoned him back and told him that I should have mentioned that I wanted her to have wings on the cover to tie in with the theme and title of the issue, **The Sound of Her Wings**. "I already gave her wings," he said. "Didn't I tell you?" He was never able satisfactorily to explain why. Dave had used real ivy before this. But this time he used fake ivy, so wherever the original is, it still looks like this.

NG

The Sandman no. 8 cover

1989

Acrylic, ink, oil pastels, wooden frame, plastic ivy

24 x 36 inches

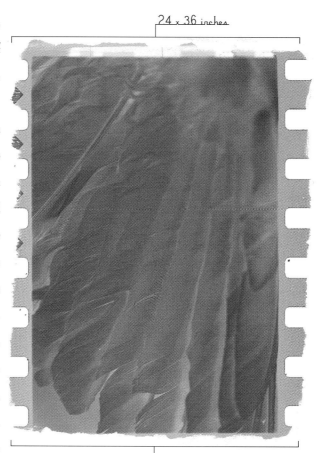

Personal photograph

1997

Photographic negative

35mm

The Doll's House began when I was nearing the end of ARKHAM ASYLUM for DC. An increasingly worried Karen Berger did not believe that I would finish it in time for its advertised release date. She thought I should stop doing the covers for HELLBLAZER and SANDMAN so that I could concentrate on getting that book done. I'd pretty much decided to give up HELLBLAZER anyway, but I really wanted to stay with SANDMAN. It was, of course, Karen's book and she could have simply given the assignment to someone else. But, instead, we had a meeting that was understanding, good-humored and diplomatic. I presented my case. She, hers. I was left with a genuine feeling of cooperation on the part of us both, and I left for England the next day. It took me 24 hours to realize I had actually been gently removed from SANDMAN during the meeting. I found myself on a 747 saying to my wife, "How did she do that?" Karen is, above all, an astoundingly efficient editor on a person-to-person level, able to convince you of anything, even to convince you that it was your idea in the first place. During the flight I roughed out what I wanted to do with the next three covers. When I arrived home, I did all three in fourteen hours through the night, finishing at seven in the morning just as Clare was getting up. I called Karen and said I had three covers sitting in front of me, did she want them? **D M**

This is how the script for SANDMAN no. 11 began:

Karen just rang me up to tell me we've lost Dave on covers for a while (i.e., at least until he finishes ARKHAM, which means we've lost him through the **Doll's House** storyline, because they ought to be a set of covers) which is really a rotten note to begin on; those deadline bells are breakin' up that old gang of ours...

STOP PRESS!

DAVE MCKEAN TO CONTINUE DOING SANDMAN COVERS UNTIL HE DROPS!

Yes, it's true! Dave McKean has already done his first two covers for SANDMAN nos. 10 &11. "It was a big decision," said Mr. McKean, 25, interviewed in his spacious Frimley home by our reporter, "but I'm sure it was the right one. So what was Karen going to do? Throw them away?"

Our eyewitness reporter claims that these are two of the best covers that the title has had so far. Stay tuned for further developments. **N G**

The Doll's House collection paperback front cover

1 9 9 5

Acrylic, ink, photography, gold leaf, Mac

14 x 20 inches

The Doll's House collection interior illustration

1 9 9 6

Photography, acrylic, paper collage, Mac

300 x 800 pixels

9. This is my painting. It hangs on my stairs. I own it more or less by default. Dave offered me any one of the first nine paintings, and this was the one least likely to collapse, rust, dissolve or fall off the wall, and the one Dave was happiest to see go away. A few years later Dave read an interview with me in which I said that the original **Doll's House** trade paperback cover was my favorite, and he gave it to me, as a birthday present.

11. This was stolen, which hurt Dave more because it was his favorite. These covers were made "life-size," a change from the hugeness of the first nine. Neil Jones returns.

12. SANDMAN was a very traditional sort of comic. This is what Dr. Fredric Wertham called, in his definitive book on traditional comics, **The Seduction of the Innocent**, "the injury to the eye motif." **NG**

The Sandman no. 9 cover

1989, 1997

Acrylic, ink, photography, Mac

2580 x 3160 pixels

The Doll's House collection interior illustration

1996

Photography, acrylic, paper collage, Mac

1265 x 1934 pixels

Number 10, the model is Cathy Peters,
now wife of Neil Jones who modeled
for no. 11 with Cathy's hand (two
friends from art school, now running
The Design Umbrella). The butterfly is
from Maxilla and Mandible in New
York (highly recommended browse).
No. 13 and 14 are modeled by Neil
(Gaiman this time — now you know
why he wears shades all the time). No.
15 is Clare with a spider that had
walked across some Cellotape in my
studio, got stuck in mid-stride (do
spiders stride?), starved to death, and
was ossified by the time I found him.

DM

The Sandman no. 10 cover

1990

Acrylic, ink, photography, fishing flies

8 x 11 inches

The Doll's House collection interior illustration

1995

Photography, acrylic, paper collage, Mac

1800 x 2400 pixels

The Sandman no. 11 cover

1990

Acrylic, ink, photography, scissors, tin, butterfly

8 x 11 inches

The Doll's House collection interior illustration

1995

Photography, acrylic, paper collage, Mac

1500 x 2400 pixels

The Sandman no. 12 cover

1990

Acrylic, photography, doll, skull, pins

8 x 11 inches

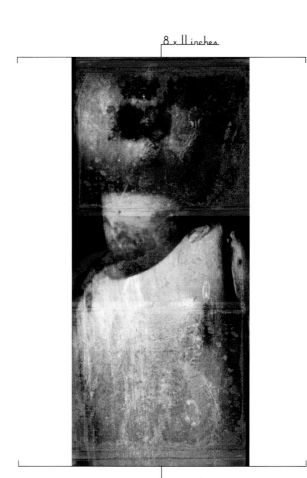

The Doll's House collection interior illustration

1995

Photography, acrylic, paper collage, Mac

1400 x 2400 pixels

The Sandman no. 13 cover

1990

Inks, photography, paper, watch

8 x 11 inches

The Doll's House collection interior illustration

1995

Photography, acrylic, paper collage, Mac

2000 x 2400 pixels

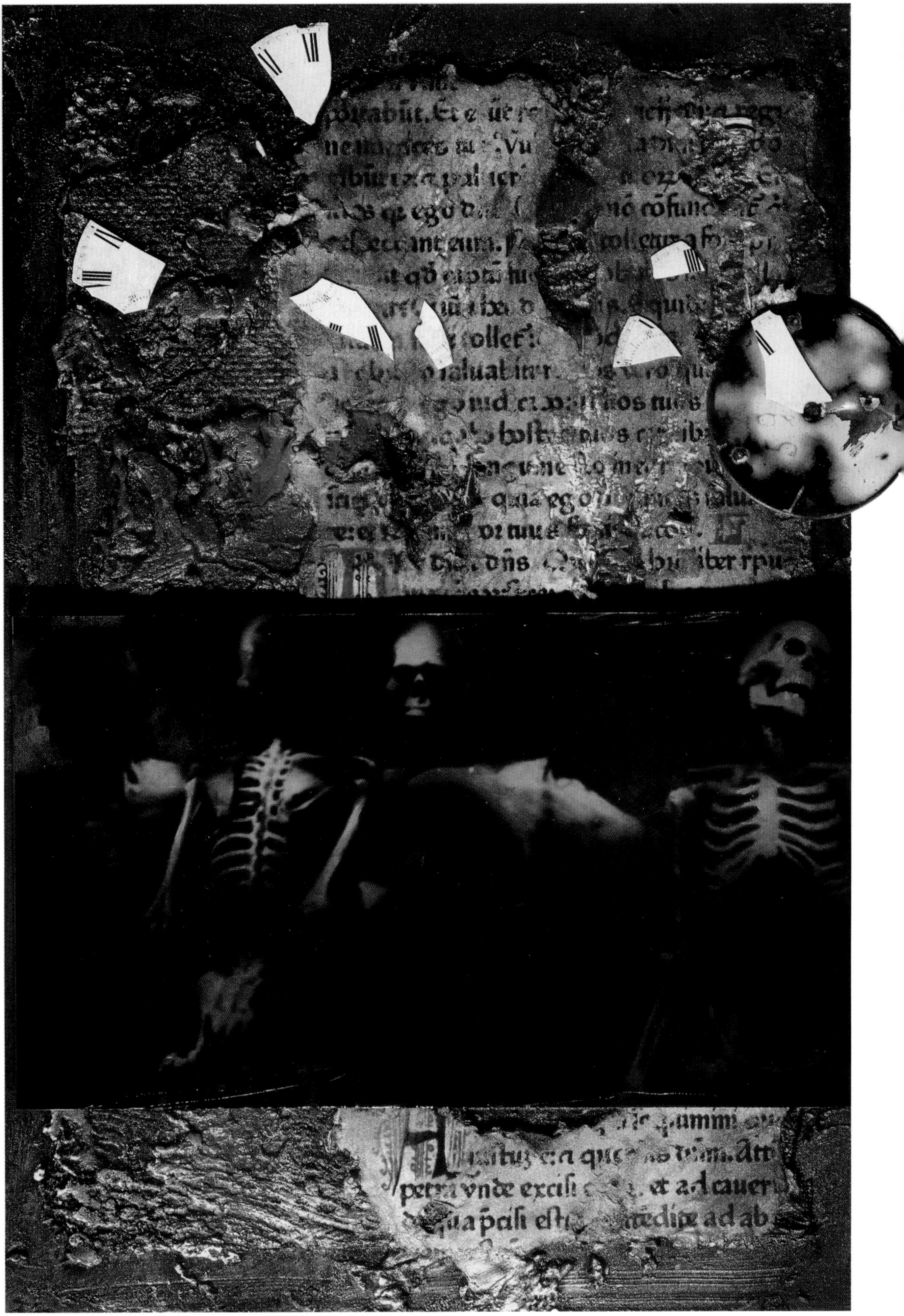

The Sandman no. 14 cover

1990

Inks, photography, paper, color xerography

8 x 11 inches

The Doll's House collection interior illustration

1995

Photography, acrylic, paper collage, Mac

1680 x 2000 pixels

The Sandman no. 15 cover

1990

Inks, photography, lace, spider, caddis fly

8 x 11 inches

The Doll's House collection interior illustration

1995

Photography, acrylic, paper collage, Mac

1680 x 1900 pixels

Since many people seemed to like the cover for no. 16 but had trouble deciding what they were looking at (a painting? a photograph?), I started saying that I'd shot a roll of twenty-four 35mm. black-and-white photos as reference for the cover, and when they were developed, the negative numbered twenty-five had this image on it. I printed it up and used it, deciding not to think too deeply about how it got there.

The truth is it's a photo of Neil sitting in my living room. Oddly enough, the first explanation actually sounds more plausible. **D M**   16. All I remember about this was how cold it was. I wanted DC to do this as a poster, but they never did. **N G**

The Sandman no. 16 cover

1990

Photography, collage

8 x 11 inches

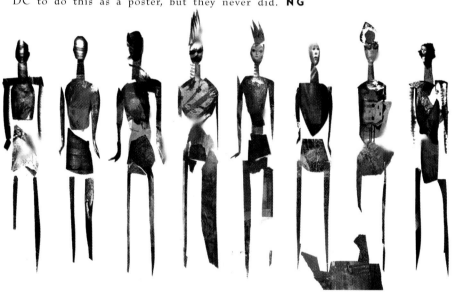

The Doll's House collection interior illustration

1995

Photography, acrylic, paper collage, Mac

4800 x 2000 pixels

The four **Dream Country** covers, together with the paperback edition cover, were most influenced by a brilliant and skewed illustrator and teacher called Barron Storey, who is known to comics readers through **Watch** magazine and his journal **MaratSade** published by Tundra/Kitchen Sink, and to the rest of the world through **Time** covers, and hundreds of album, book, and editorial illustrations. While on a signing tour for ARKHAM ASYLUM, I was fortunate enough to meet Barron in San Francisco at a gallery show of his work. The walls were covered with absurdly detailed and patterned panels, and then one room was devoted to his sketchbooks or "journals." These consisted of page after page of completely fully realized drawings and paintings, again fractally detailed, the cumulative effect of which was to convince you that no one person in one lifetime could have made ALL THESE MARKS!

I've since talked to Barron reasonably regularly and his influence remains, but at the time the impression he made on my work was obvious, actually too obvious. Nevertheless, I'm still fond of the **Facade** cover, which now hangs in my mother's house, looking a bit out of sorts surrounded by colored glass ornaments and brass bits on the mantle. **D M**

Dream Country collection paperback cover

1991

Acrylic, willow

30 x 20 inches

17. And, with the **Dream Country** covers, it was time to reinvent ourselves again. These four pointillist paintings were, I think, partly Dave's homage to Barron Storey, and partly a moving on from the photo-montages of **The Doll's House**. With each set of covers Dave would set "the rules" (I'd make suggestions, but most of the rules were Dave's) — here it was the painting style, and incorporating the title of the story into the cover.

18. There's a bird's skull on the frame, painted gold. I would tell you the story of the bird's skull, but I am still sworn to secrecy.

Dream Country collection interior illustration

1991

Pencil, ink

3 x 5 inches

19. Many strange things happened to this issue (including a misprinted version, its use in an honest-to-goodness murder and winning The World Fantasy Award). Dave won the World Fantasy Award as Best Artist the year this won Best Short Story, for the body of covers that year.

20. I love this cover. **N G**

The Sandman no. 17 cover

1990

Acrylic, inks, varnish, peacock feathers

18 x 24 inches

Dream Country collection interior illustration

1991

Pencil, inks

8 x 10 inches

The Sandman no. 18 cover

1990

Acrylic, inks, varnish, oil pastels, frames, bird skull

18 x 24 inches

Dream Country collection interior illustration

1991

Pencil, inks

8 x 10 inches

The Sandman no. 19 cover

1990

Acrylic, inks, varnish, paper

18 x 24 inches

Dream Country collection interior illustration

1991

Pencil, inks

8 x 10 inches

The Sandman no. 20 cover

1990

Acrylic, inks, leaves

18 x 24 inches

Dream Country collection interior illustration

1991

Pencil, inks [includes Arvo Pärt's signature]

8 x 10 inches

I must admit I don't remember much in the way of anecdote or purpose with these covers.

I do remember being happy with the way the type worked with the compositions.

I remember the boy in the photographs on no. 26 was an old snap of Clare's father Garth, age 10.

But most of all I remember Karen Berger asking me in San Diego what the next series of covers was going to look like. I think I was late with the first one already so I should have known. I remember doing a ratty doodle of something or other on a paper napkin. I think I scribbled the words Season of Mists halfheartedly around the three-quarter mark. After another glass of wine I improvised and gesticulated and generally flailed for about five minutes or so. I'm sure Karen knew I was making it up as I went along, but, either out of a profound trust in my ability to deliver the goods, or a reluctance to watch me flounder pathetically around my tortured little biro thumbnail any longer than absolutely necessary, she smiled kindly; "Sounds good," she lied. "Have a prawn." **DM**

p a p e r n a p k i n

Personal photograph

1995

Photography

8 x 10 inches

Season of Mists collection paperback [front cover [detail]

21. And in the blink of an eye, we reinvent ourselves once more. I remember only Dave showing me, with a ballpoint pen on a scrap of paper, what the Season of Mists covers would look like, showing me the new cover, the new logo, the typography, the way the S and M of Season of Mists would overlay the SANDMAN logo. By the time he had finished I had no clue what the new covers would look like. "Sounds brilliant," I said, figuring it would be. **N G**

s c r **1992** p o f p a p e r

Photography, acrylic, collage, clay

28 x 18 inches

22. I forget why Nada was on the cover of this chapter. Probably because she wasn't inside.

23. Based on the cover of SANDMAN no. 4.

25. If you're the writer, people ask you to sign the covers of their comics. If you're me you tend to dot the eyes (which Dave wishes I wouldn't, but, as I point out to him, there are still going to be 98,000 copies out there I *haven't* defaced, and it keeps me interested while I sign). I only mention this because I discovered that a little gold or silver on the eyes of any of the nine images on this cover renders it amazingly creepy.

26. Note the fish at the top of the key. [I had to change this one, it was just too bad to see print with its original fish] **D M**

28. For some reason the colors in this cover when reproduced were very odd. The border is made of beaten copper foil and is copper-colored, not the bright yellow it appeared on the cover. **N G**

The Sandman no. 21 cover

1990

Photography, collage

8 x 10 inches

Personal photography

1997

Photographic negative

35mm

The Sandman no. 22 cover

1990

Photography, collage, negative

8 x 10 inches

Personal photography

1997

Photographic negative

35mm

SEASON OF MISTS

The Sandman no. 23 cover

1990

Photography, collage, acrylic, copper, pomegranate

10 x 14 inches

Personal photography

1997

Photographic negative

35mm

The Sandman no. 24 cover

1990, 1997

Photography, collage, acrylic, Mac

2200 x 2300 pixels

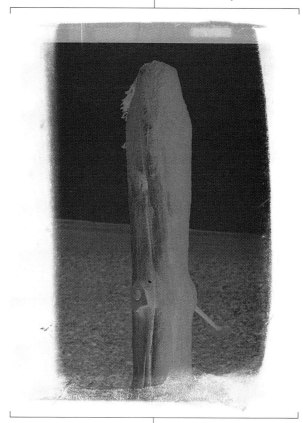

Personal photography

1997

Photographic negative

35mm

THE DREAMLINES, DRIFTER'S PARTING GIFT, ATTRACTS UNWANTED ATTENTION; AND THE DREAM LORD RECEIVES UNWELCOME VISITORS.

The Sandman no. 25 cover

1990

Photography, collage

2200 x 2800 pixels

Personal photography

1997

Photographic negative

35mm

The Sandman no. 26 cover

1990, 1997

Photography, collage, shell, cogs, Mac

10 x 14 inches

Personal photography

1997

Photographic negative

35mm

The Sandman no. 27 cover

1991

Photography, collage, acrylic

8 x 10 inches

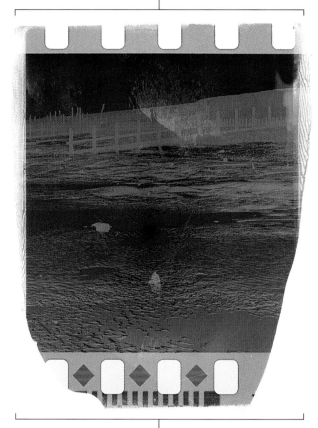

Personal photography

1997

Photographic negative

35mm

The Sandman no. 28 cover

1991

Acrylic on photographs, color xerography, copper

10 x 14 inches

Personal photography

1997

Photographic negative

35mm

I had completely forgotten where these covers came from until I started talking to Neil about what sort of anecdotes to write for this book. Neil showed me a series of Shakespeare book covers by Milton Glaser that featured generically monochrome drawings with limited watercolor details. The first is, I suppose, in the style of early Brad Holland, a huge influence on me at art school, partly for his extraordinary draftsmanship, but mostly for his ability to navigate perfectly between a melancholy seriousness and a thoughtful warm humor in his work, a skill that almost always eludes me. The second is definitely Beardsley, who I'm not a fan of particularly, but seemed appropriate. The last is in the style I was working on for **Cages**, my own "graphic novel" (fat comic), published by Kitchen Sink. **D ⅲ**

Personal drawing

1997

Ink

8 x 10 inches

The Sandman no. 30 cover detail

1991

Acrylic

3 x 3 inches

I've been fond of the Milton Glaser covers to the Signet Shakespeares since I was given my first copies, about 25 years ago. I liked the way he painted, in vivid watercolors, small areas of otherwise black-and-white drawings, and suggested to Dave that it might be a nice approach to take for the three historical stories of **Distant Mirrors**.

29. In the printed cover of this, someone at DC replaced Dave's painted crescent moon with a flat green crescent. No one knows why to this day.

30. More moons — echoes of the fact that we were naming each episode after a month.

50. The last of the **Distant Mirrors** covers, we made it gold-and-white on black to preserve the thematic unity of the **Distant Mirrors** covers while not risking confusing people with another white cover. Or something like that. **NG**

The Sandman no. 29 cover

1991

Ink, acrylic

14 x 20 inches

Personal drawing

1997

Ink

8 x 10 inches

The Sandman no. 30 cover

1991

Ink, acrylic

14 x 20 inches

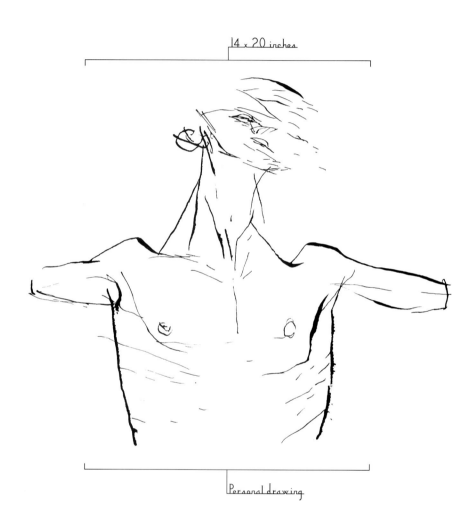

Personal drawing

1997

Ink

8 x 10 inches

The Sandman no. 31 cover

1991

Ink, acrylic

14 x 20 inches

Personal drawing

1997

Ink

8 x 10 inches

The Sandman no. 50 cover

1993

Acrylic, photography

25 x 15 inches

Personal drawing

1997

Ink

8 x 10 inches

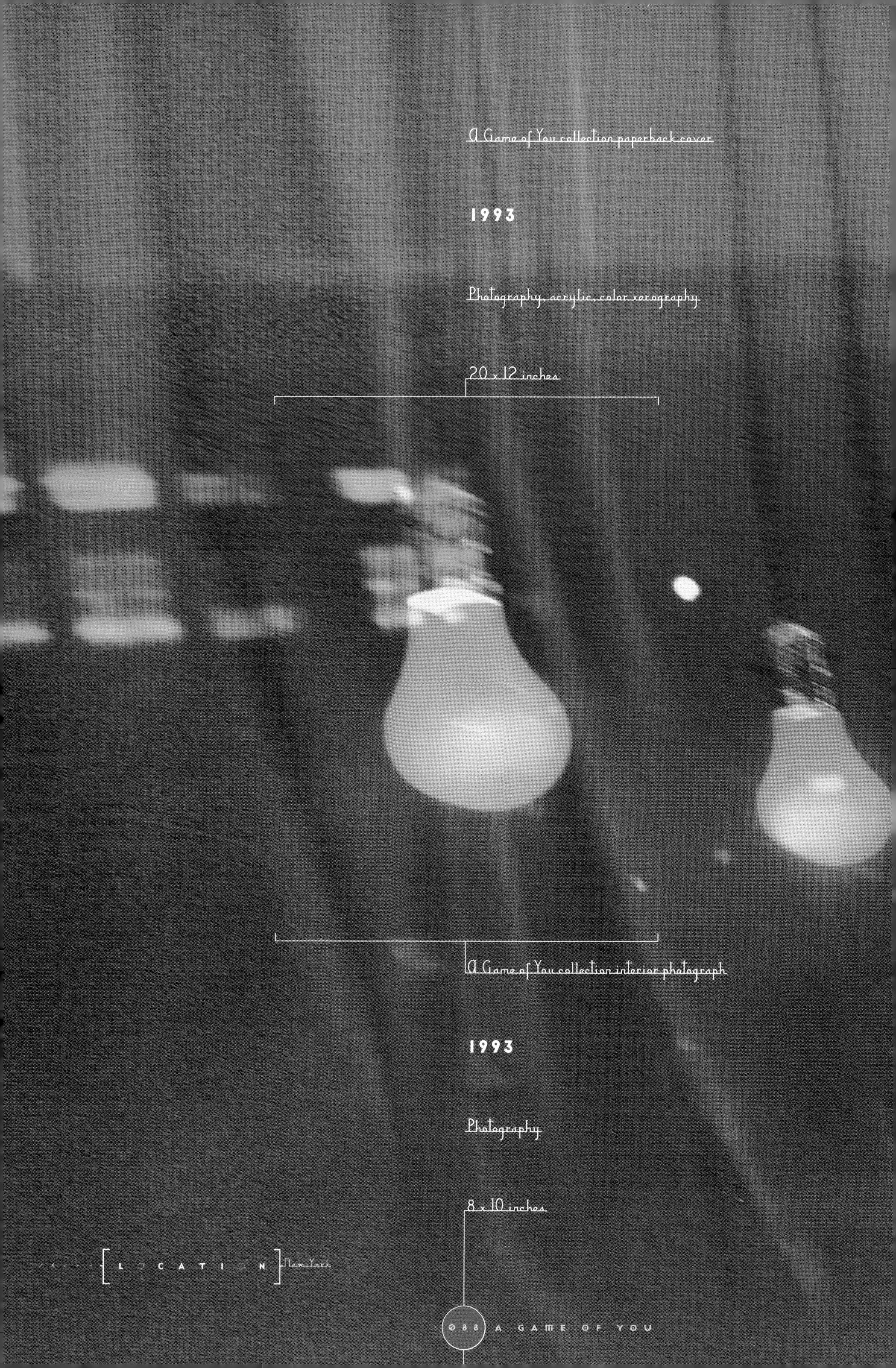

A Game of You collection paperback cover

1993

Photography, acrylic, color xerography

20 x 12 inches

A Game of You collection interior photograph

1993

Photography

8 x 10 inches

[LOCATION] New York

I remember the retailers complaining about the fact that the SANDMAN logo was in the middle of the page and no one could find their SANDMANs. I remember readers complaining that the covers were ugly, and they hated the story.

But I loved the strange, divided, part sepia-photo-construct, part real-New York covers. And, in many ways, **A Game of You,** prickly and jagged though it is, is my favorite of the SANDMAN storylines. Sorry. **N G**

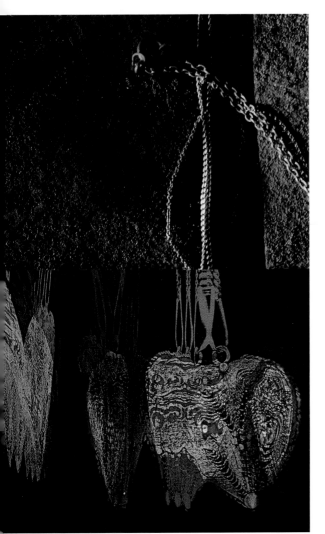

The **A Game of You** covers were generally disliked as far as I can make out. The hard, incongruous half-and-half composition was thought by many not to work. The retailers hated the logo being so far down on the cover. DC didn't like the A GAME OF YOU type disappearing into the background.

They are still some of my personal favorites.

These photographic experiments produced a way of working that I've applied to all sorts of CD and personal projects since.

I finally got to use some of the photos I took of New York during my first visit to the U.S. in the summer of 1986. (When I visited DC to show my portfolio to whoever I could find, Andy Helfer showed interest in my work but never got back to me. He claims to have forgotten about this completely. Hi Andy.)

I also continued experimenting with color photocopiers for the top half of each piece. During my time working on **Signal to Noise**, again with that man Gaiman, I took over a copy shop in Camberley where I lived at the time and forced this poor machine against its will to do things it was never designed for.

The composition obviously reflected the two worlds running parallel throughout the story. As final defense, all I can say is, controversial or not, commercially insensitive design or not, the sales of SANDMAN continued to rise throughout the storyline, and my trust in SANDMAN readers to find each issue whether it was immediately obvious on the stands or not seemed to be validated. **D m**

The Sandman no. 32 cover

1992

Photography, collage, color xerography

8 x 11 inches

A Game of You collection interior photograph

1993

Photography

7 x 10 inches

A GAME OF YOU

The Sandman no. 33 cover

1992

Photography, collage, color xerography

8 x 11 inches

A Game of You collection interior photograph

1993

Photography

7 x 10 inches

The Sandman no. 34 cover

1992

Photography, collage, color xerography

8 x 11 inches

A Game of You collection interior photograph

1993

Photography

7 x 10 inches

The Sandman no. 35 cover

1992

Photography, collage, color xerography

8 x 11 inches

A Game of You collection interior photograph

1993

Photography

7 x 10 inches

a game of you

RATES

$1.10	FIRST	1/9 MILE
10¢	EACH ADDITIONAL	1/9 MILE

The Sandman no. 36 cover

1992

Photography, collage, color xerography

8 x 11 inches

A Game of You collection interior photograph

1993

Photography

7 x 10 inches

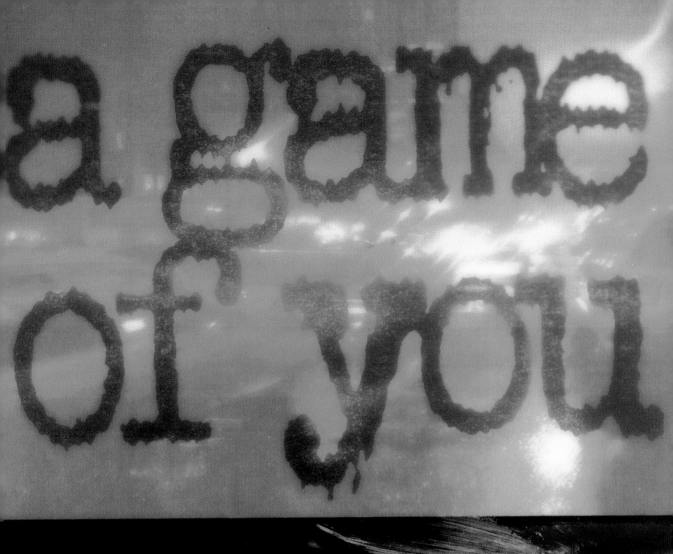

The Sandman no. 37 cover

1992

Photography, collage, color xerography

8 x 11 inches

A Game of You collection interior photograph

1993

Photography

7 x 10 inches

The **Convergence** covers were a lot of fun.

I'd always loved masks and wanted to try some more elaborate photography since I'd started shooting everything at Splash of Paint, an inspiring and unique design company run by my ex-teacher from Berkshire College of Art, Malcolm Hatton. Splash's in-house photographer Bob Watt helped me with the technical side of these shoots. Clare wore the flat painted masks and was sainterly patient. Bob's a curious character. He's slightly deaf, so you're never sure whether you are making contact with him. He takes light readings and murmurs, "Ooh. Three at two point five, three at two point five urm, ooh three, um, urm at two point five..." for what seems like hours, the atmosphere of unconfidence is almost tangible. I thought the chances of these shots coming about were nil. They were all perfect.

To date, Bob's never been wrong, yet every time the F-stop chant begins, my spirits sink. **D M**

38.

I love the illusions of these covers: the place where the photography and flat art come together. Again, pre-computers, Dave did it by making it, and then photographing it.

I think of these covers as the closest to Dave McKean personally — the photos of him and of Clare, in their own clothes, surrounded by the kind of cool and beautiful objects with which their house, and Dave's studio nearby, is filled.

40.

At the San Diego comics convention in 1991 I was given two cool things: one was a Death doll, made by John Kuramoto and Bonnie To ; the other was a tape by a Sandman fan named Tori Amos of her not-yet-released album. The doll seemed to want to go onto this cover, with the Sri Lankan puppets and the Teddy Bear. **N G**

Fables & Reflections collection hardback front cover

1993

Photography

5 x 4 inch transparency

Fables & Reflections collection interior photograph

1993

Photograph

5 x 4 inch transparency

1992

Photography

5 x 4 inch transparency

Fables & Reflections collection interior photograph

1993

Photograph

5 x 4 inch transparency

The Sandman no. 39 cover

1992

Photography

5 x 4 inch transparency

Fables & Reflections collection interior photograph

1993

Photograph

5 x 4 inch transparency

The Sandman no. 40 cover

1992

Photography

5 x 4 inch transparency

Fables & Reflections collection interior photograph

1993

Photograph

5 x 4 inch transparency

Brief Lives collection paperback front cover

1994

Photographs, acrylic, Mac

2000 x 3000 pixels

The **Brief Lives** covers happened at a time when I was really starting to notice how homogenous the aesthetic of mainstream comic covers was. Whether painted, pen and inked or whatever, the emphasis was on a standard, comic book/fantasy illo/pulp fiction quick sell. Large slick picture of main character(s) or big realistic face close-up or...you get the idea. "Here's everything in your face, get it? Huh? Get it?"

I thought I'd do a series of "little things" covers. Small details, fractured bits of type, the detritus that might be collected along the way, during this Sandman/Delirium road-story. We had a fifth metallic ink to play with, and I tried eight times to get the translucent metallic ink I wanted. We finally got the right effect, if not the right ink, by printing the fifth color underneath the four-color image.

Actually, since I mention pulp fiction (the genre, not the movie), I should mention the case of the disappearing nipple. Number 45 originally had a nipple on the cover, top left. I don't know what I was thinking. Karen spotted it immediately, and the nipple was brought before Dick Giordano, VP and Editor of...well...Nipples, to make a decision, and would you believe it oh my little brothers, the nipple was axed, cut, edited and removed. Replaced in fact with a bit of blue. Sad but true.

But look, the case has a happy ending, because it's now 1997, and times a-change. In the anything-goes pages of Vertigo, nipples are a dime a dozen. In fact you're more likely to run into problems if you don't include a scattering of assorted nudie bits in each issue. So here is the unexpurgated [and enhanced] version. **D M**

Brief Lives collection interior photograph

1994

Photography

5 x 4 inch transparency

41. The chapter titles of **Brief Lives** were tiny, dislocated phrases, quotes from or comments upon the events of the chapter in question. That was reflected in the covers — strange, bitty, each composed, more or less, of six squares, a strip down the side, and a number in the top right corner; and over those, often in the fifth color ink we'd be using, the title fragments would be printed. If anyone asked us we said it was art, but mostly it was too much fun. **N G**

The Sandman no. 41 cover

1992

Photographs, resin, dried flowers, book, nails, picture frame, collage

10 x 15 inches

Brief Lives collection interior photograph

1994

Photography

5 x 4 inch Transparency

The Sandman no. 42 cover

1992

Photographs, type, photocopies, acrylic

10 x 15 inches

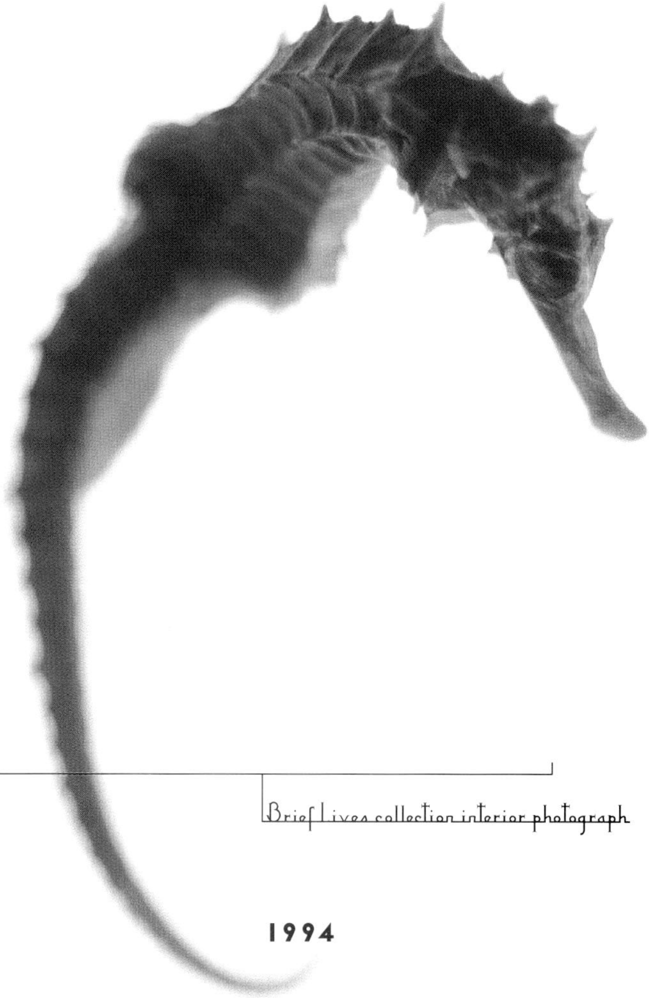

Brief Lives collection interior photograph

1994

Photography

5 x 4 inch transparency

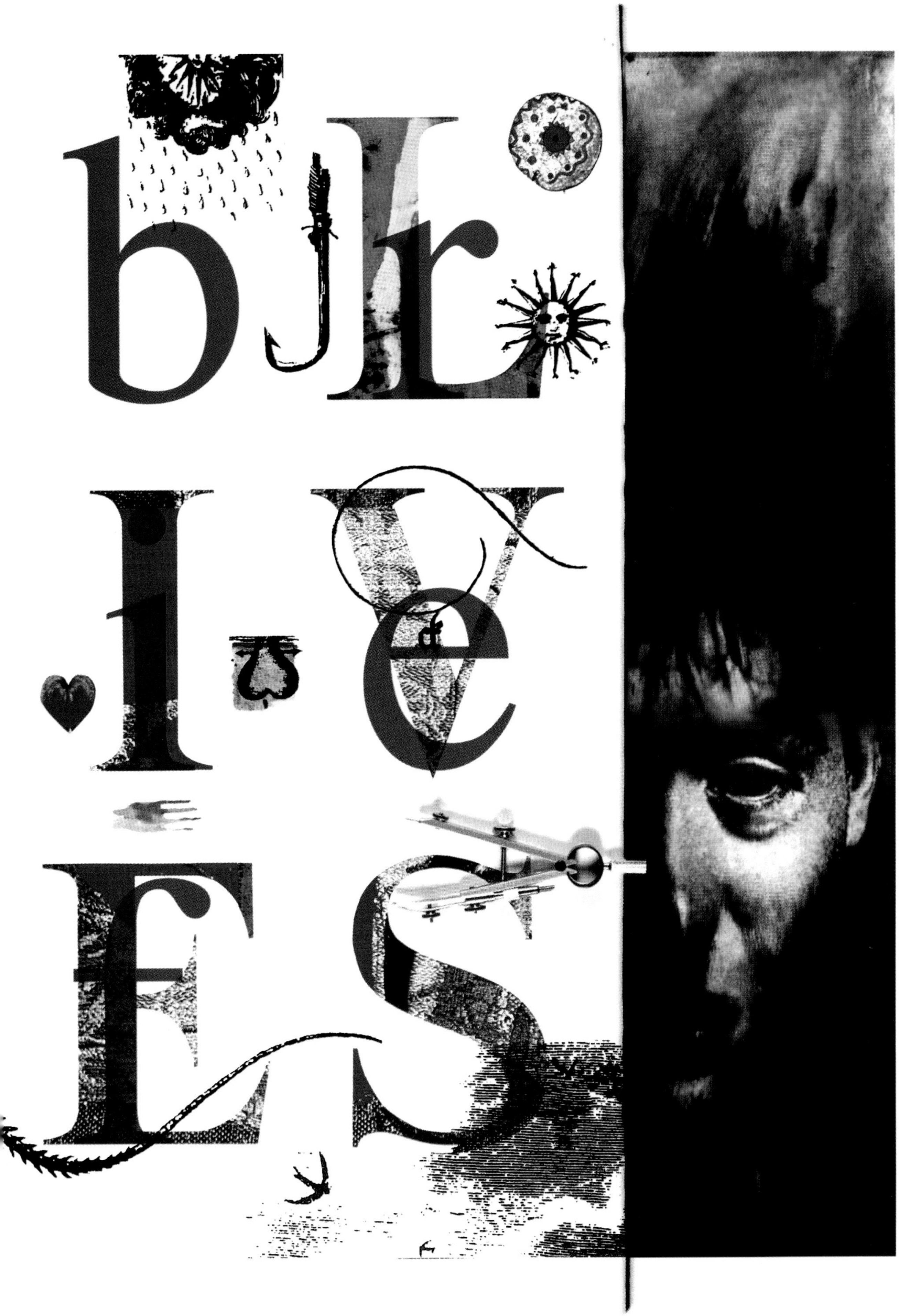

43. I still wonder what kind of
insect the doll is holding. **NG**

The Sandman no. 43 cover

1992

Acrylic, insect, copper dust, gold leaf

8 x 11 inches

Brief Lives collection interior photograph

1994

Photography

5 x 4 inch transparency

The Sandman no. 44 cover

1992

Acrylic, color xerography

20 x 32 inches

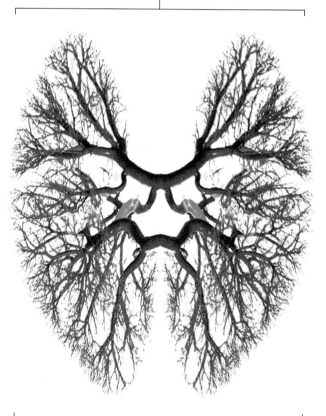

Brief Lives collection interior photograph

1994

Photography

5 x 4 inch transparency

45. What was odd about this, our only censored cover, is that the original (with nipple) was printed not only as a trading card, but also in the various other countries that reprint SANDMAN, and no one has ever noticed. The story was conceived during Kevin Eastman's stag night, which was celebrated in a local strip joint. I watched the dancers for the first ten minutes, watched the customers for the next ten, then amused myself for the following three hours by bringing SANDMAN characters in, in my head, and finally in destroying the place. **N G**

The Sandman no. 45 cover

1992

Photography, acrylic, lace, dollar bill

10 x 15 inches

Brief Lives collection interior photograph

1994

Photography

5 x 4 inch transparency

The Sandman no. 46 cover

1992

Photography, acrylic, silk, color xerography

10 x 15 inches

Brief Lives collection interior photograph

1994

Photography

5 x 4 inch transparency

47. This was the first Vertigo issue. The thing that made Vertigo issues Vertigo issues was the half-inch-wide strip down the left-hand side. Dave took this very badly, as it threw off the six-panel design for the **Brief Lives** covers. I remember him offering all kinds of sensible aesthetic reasons for not getting the strip on the SANDMAN covers until we were done with **Brief Lives**. He failed. After a while, though, the left-hand-side strip became nominal, and then completely imaginary. **NG**

The Sandman no. 47 cover

1992

Acrylic, color xerography

10 x 15 inches

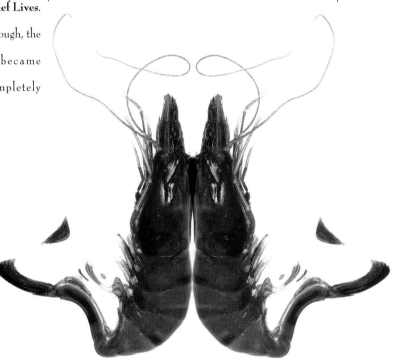

Brief Lives collection interior photograph

1994

Photography

5 x 4 inch transparency

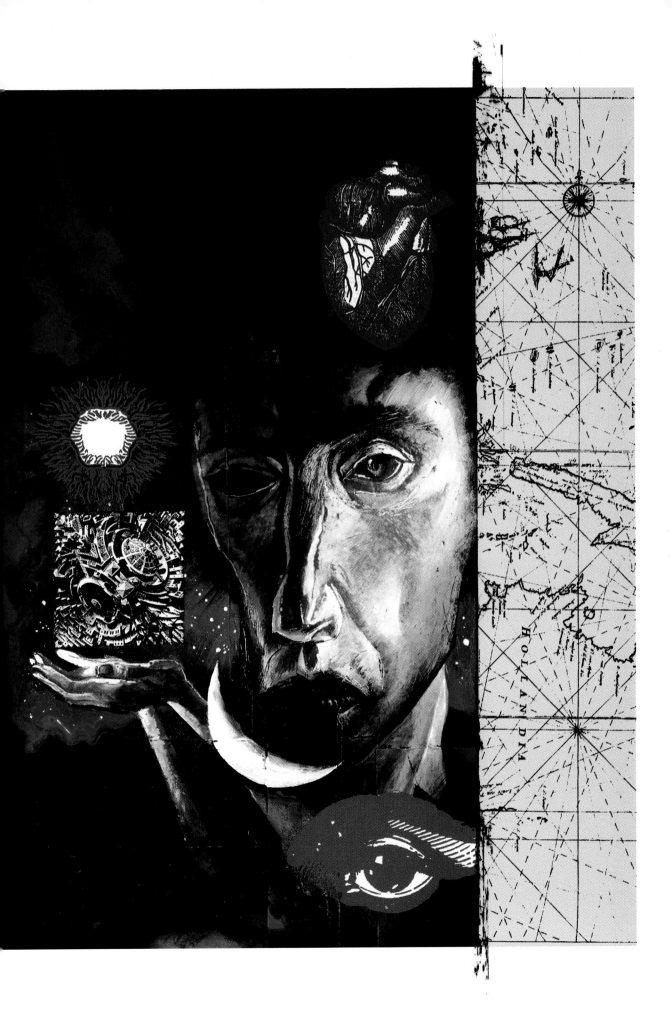

The Sandman no. 48 cover

1992

Acrylic, color xerography, cutlery

10 x 15 inches

Brief Lives collection interior photograph

1994

Photography

5 x 4 inch transparency

The Sandman no. 49 cover

1992

Photography

10 x 15 inches

Brief Lives collection interior photograph

1994

Photography

5 x 4 inch transparency

My lowest point during the seventy-five SANDMAN covers.
The images in my head and the poor relations that ended up on paper
had never been further apart.

I had been doing a lot more work outside of the comics world and
generally enjoying that a lot more. But, I was very aware that my
"competition" in, for example, the record cover business were far more
skilled and disciplined designers than me and/or were computer literate.
Now, I've been an odd mix of techie and Luddite for a while now.
I saw no real contradiction in believing that computer musical
instruments and midi sequencers were wonderful aids to composition,
while
simultaneously
that if you plugged
believing
that that if you plugged p l u g g

a modem
into your home phone socket
into your home phon

that people could get into your house
at people could get into your hous

and steal things.
and steal

things.

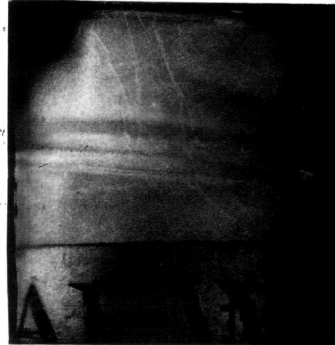

Despite my friend Neil Jones's frequent and patient attempts to
convince me that this was impossible. I was sure that even possessing
a modem, let alone a whole computer system, had a whiff of evil
about it.
So I put off the fateful day until eventually I capitulated and signed in
blood.
Obviously, the Mac is a wonderful tool, approachable and powerful.
Occasionally I wish there was a button on the side of it that says,
"Oh, you know what I mean," but generally it's been a godsend.

DM

The last three **Worlds' End** covers were faltering first attempts, but over the last two years I've come closer than ever before to realizing what until recently only flickered inside my head.

The first three were originally straight photographs. I was never happy with them, especially nos. 52 and 53, so I've reworked them from the original elements for this collection.

What else can I tell you? The inn on the cover of no. 51 is the twelfth-century Mermaid Inn in Rye. The face on no. 54 is not Jimmy Carter, and the moon on no. 56 becoming white and positive when the pub sign was inverted to a negative image was a completely unplanned happy accident. **D m**

The Sandman no. 51 cover

1993

Photography, collage, branches, ironwork

4 x 5 inch transparency

Personal photography 'Reach- Kent, England'

1994

Photography

10 x 10 inches.

51. The conceit of the Worlds' End stories was that they were tales told, in a pub, by travelers. So a pub-sign seemed like a perfect place to start. "And the moon," I told Dave. "We need the moon." I assumed it was black for a reason.

This is the first SANDMAN cover with no eyes on it anywhere.

52. Note the cover to SANDMAN no. 53, in Polaroid form.

53. Note the cover to SANDMAN no. 51, in Polaroid form.

54. My theory is that there would have been lots more Polaroids, but the unthinkable happened, and Dave bought a computer.

55. I think it was the discovery that he could make gravestones join onto skulls that sold Dave on the whole computer thing. **NG**

The Sandman no. 52 cover

1993, 1997

Photography, collage, acrylic, Mac

4 x 5 inch transparency, 2300 x 3000 pixels

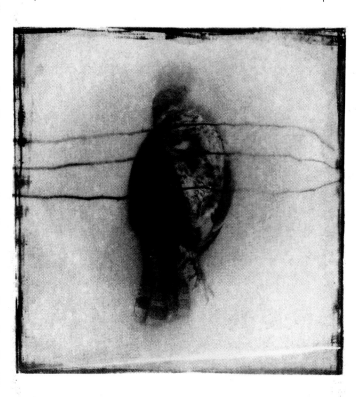

Personal photography 'Thorn-Vermont, USA'

1994

Photography

10 x 10 inches

The Sandman no. 53 cover

1993

Photography, collage, acrylic, Mac

4 x 5 inch transparency, 2300 x 3000 pixels

Personal photography 'Nightmare-Kent, England'

1994

Photography

10 x 10 inches

The Sandman no. 54 cover

1993

Photography, collage, Mac

2100 x 3000 pixels

Personal photography 'Sting-Kent, England'

1994

Photography

10 x 10 inches

The Sandman no. 55 cover

1993

Photography, collage, Mac

2100 x 3000 pixels

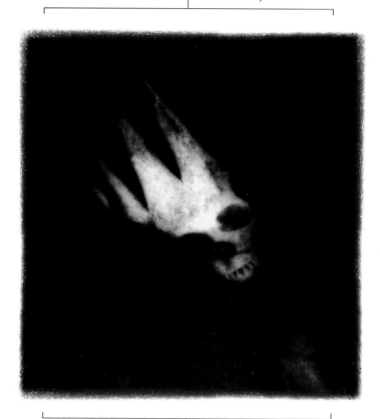

Personal photography 'King II-Kent, England'

1994

Photography

10 x 10 inches

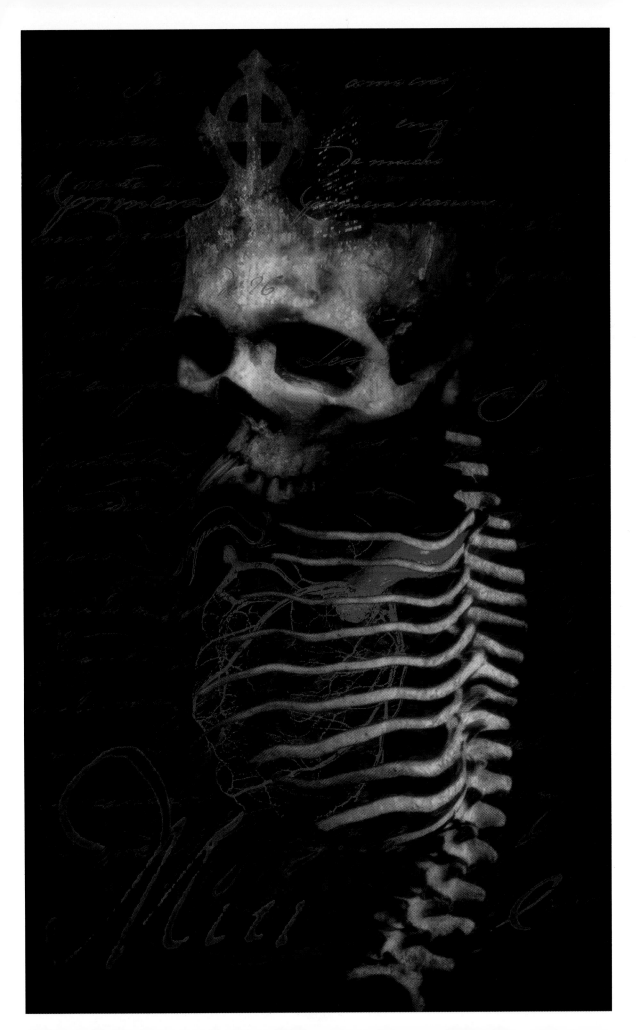

The Sandman no. 56 cover

1 9 9 3

Photography, collage, Mac

2100 x 3000 pixels

56. Look! The nega
image of the cover of n
means that the black mo
now white and glowin
knew it was black for a rea

NG

Personal photography 'Ideas-Kent, England'

1 9 9 4

Photography

10 x 10 inches

The Kindly Ones collection paperback front cover

1996

Acrylic, photography, Mac

When the **Kindly Ones** series started, something had changed. The idea of doing this collected covers book had been accepted at DC, and all of a sudden these ephemeral monthly experiments were going to be given a permanent home. **D M**

2043 x 3130 pixels

The Kindly Ones collection hardback front cover [detail]

1996

Acrylic on photograph, Mac

1317 x 1297 pixels

57 was started five times. Once with a painted composition that I liked as a doodle but just didn't work in paint. Once, with this image scanned and tri-toned and played with in the computer — still no joy. This was dumped. I told DC I was running a bit late. I got depressed and ate ice cream. I was getting a CD-ROM authored, and the guy in charge of the bureau, Simon Banton, was working on deciphering a signature on a drawing using computer-enhanced filtering. The signature looked convincingly like "Picasso." He said if he and the owner proved it was the real thing, not a middle-period Charlie Picasso for example, he was up for ten percent, but I digress...

A print of the drawing hung on the wall and was quite beautiful. I made a small sketch of an idea suggested by the drawing for a way of handling the three figures. Version three was a drawn version, version four a paint-and-photo version and finally this version, by far the best and most fun to do. The clay and wood figures are wrapped in thread, dressed in Thai silk, and collaged with sepia-toned photographs. This was lit with projected slides and photographed, scanned and touched up in Photoshop. **DM**

57. The Kindly Ones sequence was Dave's chance to cut loose with the computer, and more than the computer: to create images that did not quite accede to reason. The only thing I asked for was the cord, line, string or ribbon on the first few covers.

These were far and away the strangest of the covers. I would telephone Dave and talk at him, listing images, emotions, feelings, characters, and somewhere in the babble he would find his image.

NG

The Sandman no. 57 cover

1993

Wood and clay models, silk, photography, Mac

1860 x 2817 pixels

Personal photograph

1997

Photography

35mm

Edlen Tewrdanck entweichen sein
die on alle arbeyt die welt hat
frager·der hey\ lig geyst ist der
bey seinem lebē wiewol sich der ser krümet schon begriffen. Got
vnd die ewige

The Sandman no. 58 cover

1993

Clay and thread figure, photography, Mac

1860 x 2817 pixels

Personal photograph

1997

Photography

35mm

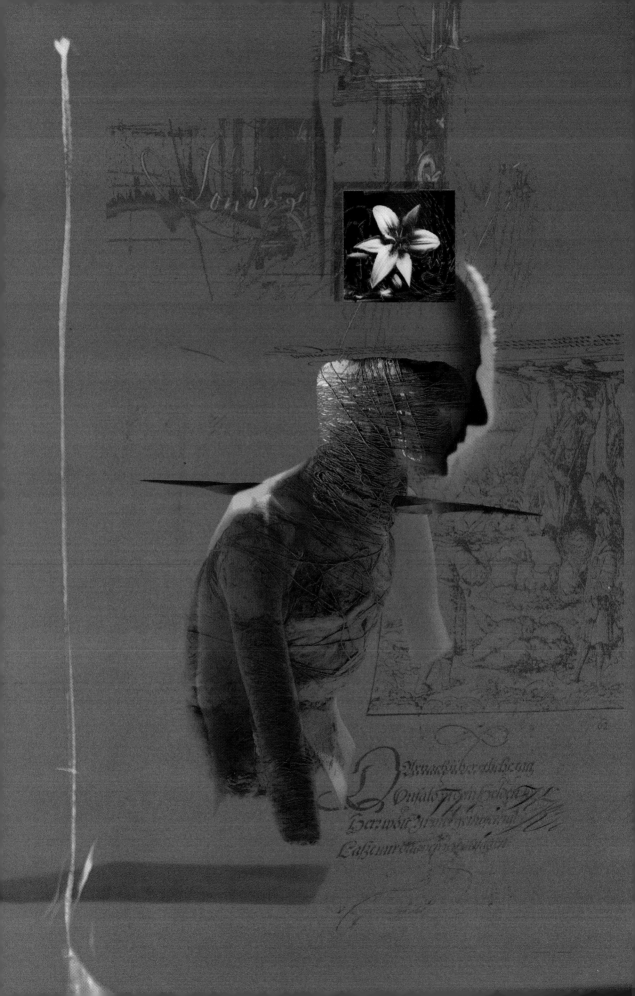

1993

Clay and thread figure, photography, Mac

58, 59. I asked Neil if he had any fish planned for the story.

Neil told me about the child in the fireplace scene for no. 58 and then three weeks later withdrew that suggestion, saying it would appear in no. 59. These two covers were done together continuing with the sculptural figures from no. 57.

At this point the prospect of a fish in the storyline looked dim, but I remained hopeful. **DM**

1860 x 2817 pixels

59. "You put some fish in this one!" said Dave when he read it — and after he had created the cover.

"Um, yes."

"Why didn't you tell me? You know I wanted to put fish on the cover. You never mentioned the fish. You just told me about the kid in the fire."

"Um. Sorry. I forgot."

"Well, don't forget next time. Fish. Yes?"

"Fish."

NG

Personal photograph

1997

Photography

35mm

1993

Silk, keys, photography, Mac

1860 x 2817 pixels

60. I'd bought these heavy keys for certain shots in MR. PUNCH, a comic I was working on at this time with Neil. Actually, some Punch props cropped up on a few of these covers. I couldn't believe Neil still hadn't included a fish in the storyline. Didn't he realize how great fish were? **D M**

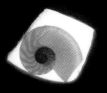

Personal photograph

1997

Photography

35mm

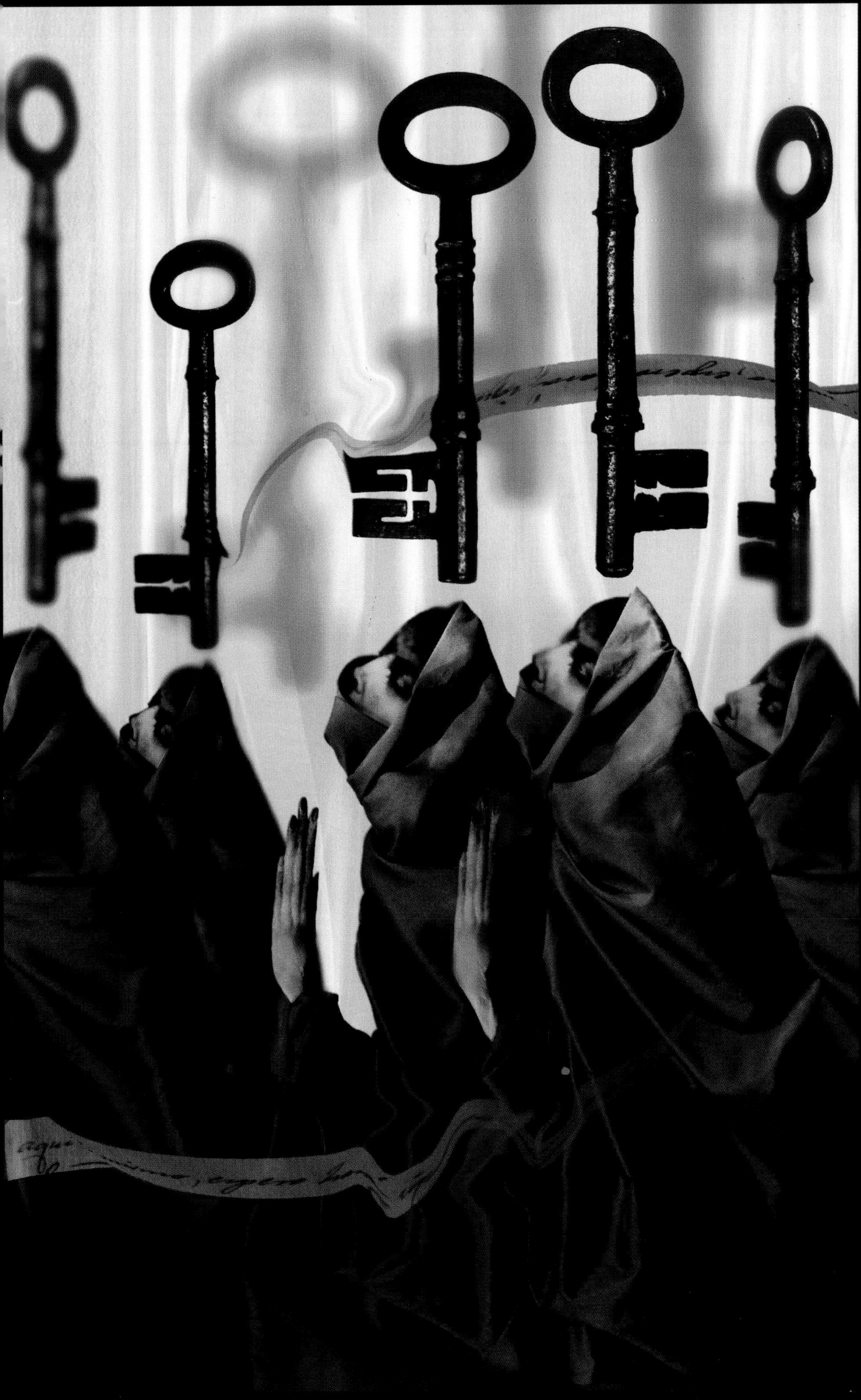

1994

Clay and thread figure, silk, microscope, photography, Mac

1860 x 2817 pixels

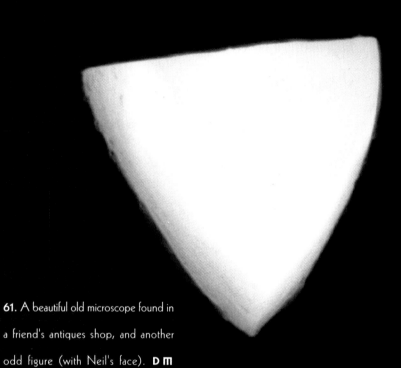

61. A beautiful old microscope found in
a friend's antiques shop, and another
odd figure (with Neil's face). **D M**

Personal photograph

1997

Photography

35mm

The Sandman no. 62 cover

1994

Photography Mac

1860 x 2817 pixels

62. Neil wanted a quote from **The
Doll's House** on this one, so I included
Cathy Peter's hand from the cover of 11.

62. This chapter was structurally a
reprise of SANDMAN no. 10. The
reason it has an image from
SANDMAN no. 11 on the cover is
that I have a rotten memory for
issue numbers and told Dave it was
a recap of SANDMAN no. 11. It's
such a pretty cover I never wanted
to cavil. Now it can be told. **N G**

Personal photograph

I'm beginning to suspect that Neil just
can't write fish. **D M**

1997

Photography

35mm

63. Neil suggested an image of snake hair. I think this is my all-time favorite SANDMAN cover. Don't know why. I was really coming to grips with the computer, and the edit on this image was a pure joy. When you make a painting or drawing you rarely get surprised by it. Certainly the odd expressive mark or texture excites you, but you rarely get the same sort of impact looking at your own work that you do looking at other people's. I worked on each element for this cover separately and then composited them very quickly at the last minute. I remember laughing out loud as they fell into place. **D M**

63. I love this one. **N G**

The Sandman no. 63 cover

1994

Clay and thread figure, photography, silk, Mac

1860 x 2817 pixels

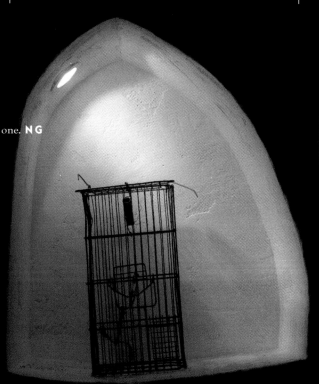

Personal photograph

1997

Photography

35mm

64. Completely gutted to find out that Neil wrote several fish into the last few issues and didn't tell me. I missed my opportunity. Depressed and disgruntled I reused some of the props from earlier covers, including the hourglass from no. 1. (Hourglass, incidentally, is the name of my design studio, taken from the short story by Bruno Schulz, **Under the Sign of the Hourglass,** and also the fact that I'm always late.) **D M**

The Sandman no. 64 cover

1994

Sand, hourglass, photography, various objects, Mac

1860 x 2817 pixels

Personal photograph

1997

Photography

35mm

The Sandman no 65 cover

1994

Clay and thread figure photography. Mac

1860 x 2817 pixels

65. This cover's most important bit is the small piece of skin that stretches below the front teeth when the lower lip is pulled down. Little things. **D M**

Personal photograph

1997

Photography

35mm

66. The cockroach was sitting on my drawing board, right in the middle of my blank drawing board, legs in the air, brown and dead. What a strange place to die. "I think I'll crawl into the middle of this brightly-colored flat space where there is absolutely no possibility of food in the hope that I die and am reborn a hundred thousand times on the cover of a comic book," it presumably thought. **D M**

The Sandman no. 66 cover

1994

Soil, cockroach, driftwood, water, ink, photography, Mac

1860 x 2817 pixels

66. I mostly remember phone calls where I'd say to Dave, for example, "Could I have a lot of blood on the next one. Maybe a puddle." And he'd say "What about a fish? I want to put some fish on the cover, you know." **N G**

Personal photograph

1997

Photography

35mm

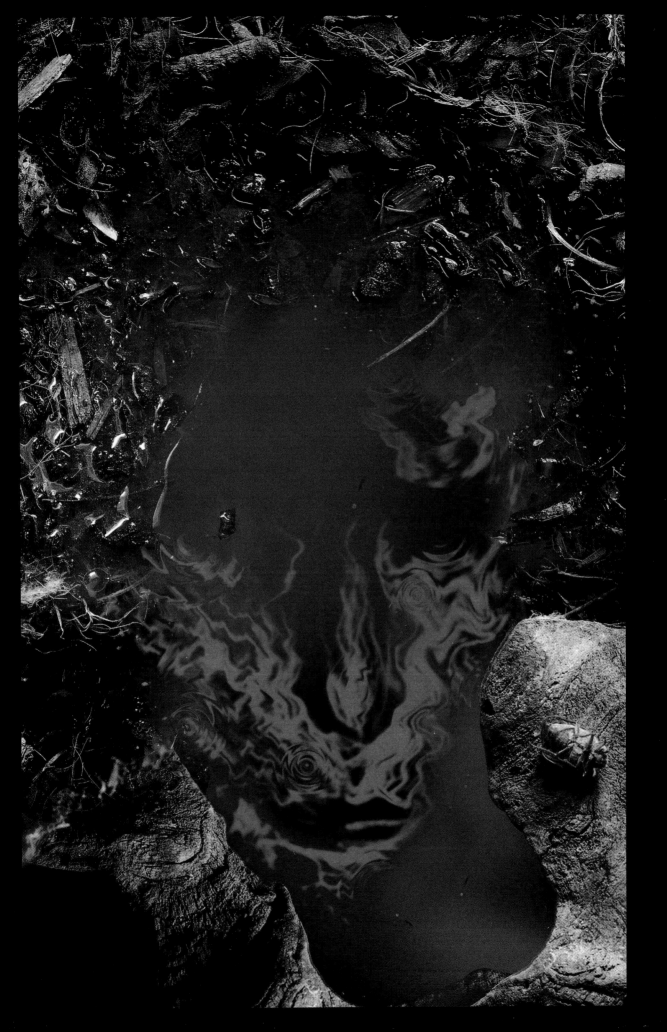

67. Stuff the writer!
I want to put a fish on the cover and
I'm GONNA put a fish on the cover,
partly because it's an important
statement I need to make, but mostly
because that bloody fish has been in
the studio too long and is stinking the
place out. Why wasn't it in the fridge,
I hear you ask? Well, who thinks of
such practicalities when you're battling
          67. I wrote a sequence with
with petulant authors and their fishless
          rainbow-minded Delirium holding
scripts! **D M**
          a fish on a string, while she spoke
to someone playing the piano, in
the issue following this one, and
forgot to mention it to Dave. Why
did he wrap this herring in string,
and place it on a music stand with
a crayon rainbow behind? Perhaps
we will never know. If it was
synchronicity, surely this cover
should have been on
SANDMAN no. 68.

Whenever I asked Dave what was
going to be on the cover of this
issue, he said it would have to be a
surprise, as he was unable to explain
it. **N G**

1994

Fish, string, paper, music stand, crayon, photography, Mac

1860 x 2817 pixels

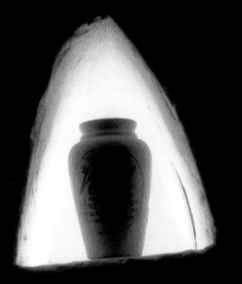

Personal photograph

1997

Photography

35mm

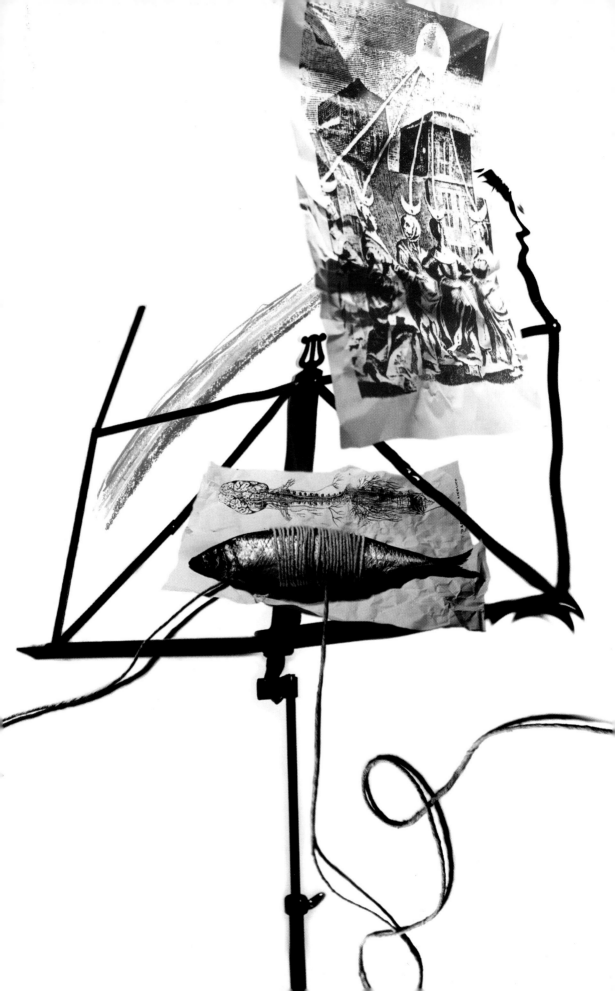

1 9 9 5

Slate, acrylic, silk, lay hand, photography, Mac

68. The really odd thing is that Neil, without seeing or hearing about the cover to no. 67, wrote a fish ON A LEASH into no. 68. There have been numerous

1860 x 2817 pixels

synchronicitous moments during the seven years of SANDMAN, but this is the unlikeliest. **D m**

Personal photograph

1 9 9 7

Photography

3.5mm

1995

69. The background is an old fireplace
and a typesetter's tray. Both were doused
with petrol one winter morning and
ritualistically set on fire.

An important moment, I think. **D M**

Burnt type tray, clay figure, silk, photography, Mac

1860 x 2817 pixels

69. The end of the ribbon that
began at the start of The Kindly
Ones. **N G**

Personal photograph

1997

Photography

35mm

What a strange feeling.

 Like a friend coming to stay for a long time, so long that you planned all sorts of things to do and see, so long that you wondered what you'd do with all the evenings, and secretly wondered if you'd get bored with each other's company. And then suddenly you only have one week left, and then a couple of days, and then they're gone, so much undone. I find myself at the airport saying, "I was sure we were going to repaint the Sistine Chapel while you were here."

Oh well, a final few words. Single objects against flat color backgrounds; a clay torso with superimposed wet soil details, a slow-shutter image of my wife making a candlelight heart in a black room; a tiny dead baby bird, found on the steps of Rye Art, my local gallery and creative hub of the Cinq Ports; a request from Neil, a quote from the cover of no. 13, a skull from the dancing skeletons, adorned with russ leaves and ballpoint pen crosses; a chrysanthemum, its petals blended with eyes for the world awakening. **D ꟿ**

The Wake collection hardback cover

1996

Photography, iris, pen, Mac

1727 x 2319 pixels

The idea for **The Wake** covers was one of simplicity, the calm after the storm. Even so, none of the four images is quite as simple as at first it seems... **N G**

The Wake collection interior photograph [unused]

1996

Photography, Mac

900 x 900 pixels

The Wake collection paperback front cover

1996

Photography, ink drawing, antique knife, plaster sculpture, Mac

1400 x 1800 pixels, drawing 8 x 10 inches

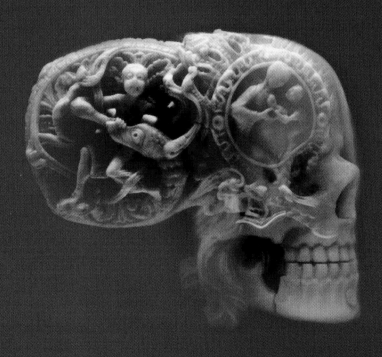

The Wake collection paperback back cover

1996

Photography, ivory carvings, Mac

1680 x 1200 pixels

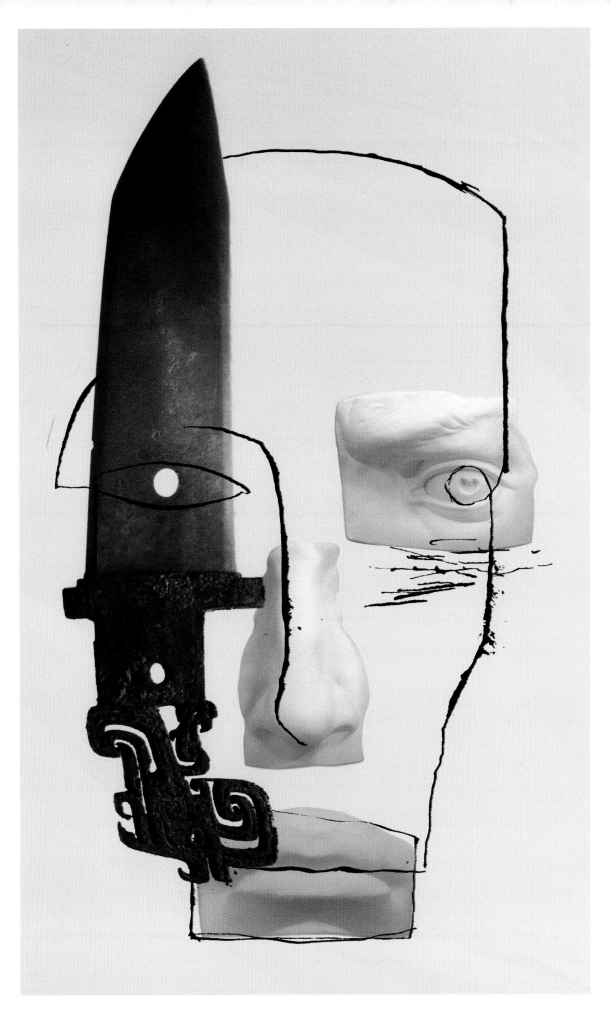

The Sandman no. 70 cover

1996

Photography, clay sculpture, paper

1211 x 1500 pixels

The Wake collection interior photograph

1996

Photography, Mac

1881 x 2046 pixels

The Sandman no. 71 cover

1996

Photography, rusty metal, dead bird, Mac

1881 x 2046 pixels

The Wake collection interior photograph

1996

Photography, Mac

726 x 831 pixels

The Sandman no. 72 cover

1996

Photography, chrysanthemum, Mac

1731 x 1641 pixels

The Wake collection interior photograph

1996

Photography, Mac

1406 x 1800 pixels

The Wake collection interior photograph

1996

Photography, Mac

1076 x 2536 pixels

The Sandman no. 73 cover

1996

Photography, plastic skull, acrylic, ink, russ leaves, Mac

1881 x 2046 pixels

The final two covers proved to be major production numbers. The cover for no. 74 includes a cup and jug contributed by Jon J Muth, the artist on that particular issue.

I composited the figure image together in the computer and made "di-sublimation" prints from them (a digital process where dyes are... um... sublimated and sealed, creating a photographic quality print).

I intended to mount the prints in a distressed wooden frame and seal them in resin while adding copper dust and earth as it hardened, and one cold January afternoon that's exactly what I did, and it looked wonderful for about twenty-five minutes. Then the resin melted the print sealant, chemically reacted with the dyes, and exploded. You see? They don't teach you this stuff at art school. How to draw pot plants and use the liquid wax machine, sure, but anything on the consequences of mixing digital prints with embedding resin? I should cocoa.

Number 75 consists of a large (6 ft.) graphite drawing smothered in soil and varnish which wouldn't dry, and an antique sewing table handed down through the generations of my wife's infinite family. The drawing dripped gloopy varnish puddles on the floor of the photographer's (Pinpoint) who I'm sure were more pissed off at me than they appeared.

Other pieces here include the covers for the three "gallery" comics, collections of single illustrations on a theme, the piece I did for my gallery show at Four Color Images in New York which included various SANDMAN covers and the large painted version of the cover of no. 35 which I completed as a centerpiece for that exhibition. Also included is the cover for Micheál Ó Súilleabháin's CD **Gaiseadh/Flowing** because it is a Sandman-inspired image, because Micheál's previous CD was my first music industry commission, and the A&R man responsible, Declan Colgan, knew my stuff through SANDMAN, and because, like the cover for no. 74, this piece also had an explosive pastlife. **D M**

The Sandman Gallery No. 1 front cover

1994

Photography, dried plants, rusted metal frame, clay mask, Mac

2100 x 3000 pixels

The Tip of My Tongue exhibition image

1995

Photography, acrylic, cactus, Mac

1500 x 1500 pixels

74. Jon Muth and Dave McKean are old friends, and there was talk at one time of letting this be the only collaborative cover in the whole SANDMAN run. Instead, Jon sent Dave things which Dave placed into this deceptive image. I was thrilled to discover that you can pull all the ad pages out of this comic, leaving the story entirely untouched.

75. The last time I was in Dave's studio (see the covers of SANDMAN no.'s 38, 39, and 40 for a visual of Dave's studio) I found the Sandman portrait part of this image propped up against a wall. It was huge, almost as big as the wall it leant against, and covered with thick, blobby varnish. I have looked all around his studio for the city on the tabletop, but I have not seen it yet.

Sandman Special 1

At the time, glow-in-the-dark covers were the Ultimate Marketing Ploy, and we were asked if we could do a glow-in-the-dark cover. So we did.

Unfortunately, someone, somewhere, forgot to tell anyone about this Ultimate Marketing Ploy, or to advertise it anywhere, so to this day I get shaken people coming up to me, their nerves shot and their fingers a-tremble, with tales of the night they saw The Face staring up at them from the darkness of their bedroom floor.

Of course, we don't have glow-in-the-dark ink in Dust Covers. So any glowing faces that stare at you from the darkness from here on are your responsibility, not ours.

NG

The Sandman no. 74 cover

1996

Photography, resin, copper dust, soil, wooden frame, nails, paper, Mac

14 x 20 inches

Personal photography

1995

Photography, resin, copper dust, soil, starfish

20 x 20 inches

The Sandman no. 75 cover

1996

Graphite, acrylic, inks, varnish, photography, antique table, Mac

2100 x 3000 pixels, 4 x 5 inch transparency, drawing: 50 x 80 inch

Personal photography

1997

Photography

6 x 8 cm transparency

The Endless Gallery front cover

1995

Acrylic, photography, book, skull, mushroom, Mac

2100 x 3000 pixels

The Endless Gallery back cover

1995

Photography

6 x 6 inches

Vertigo Gallery front cover

1995

Acrylic, photography, rose stems, color bars, Mac

2100 x 3000 pixels

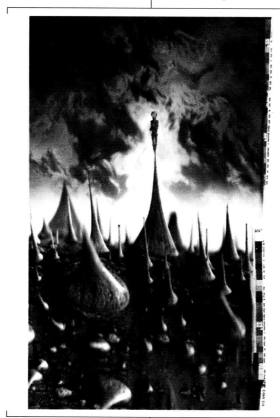

Vertigo Gallery back cover

1995

Photography, rose stem, color bars, Mac

2100 x 3000 pixels

The Sandman Special no. 1

1992, 1997

Acrylic, photography, Mac

2300 x 3200 pixels

Painting [or exhibition [version of The Sandman no. 35 cover]

1995

Acrylic on photographs, varnish, soil, rusted bed springs

46 x 36 inches

Mícheál Ó Súilleabháin–Lumen CD cover

1995

Acrylic on photographs, Mac

3000 x 3000 pixels

Mícheál Ó Súilleabháin–Gaiseadh/Flowing CD cover

1992

Photography, resin, paper collage, copper dust, slate

12 x 7 inches

Disincarnate—Dreams of the Carrion Kind CD cover

1992

Acrylic on photographs, color xerography, objects

24 x 36 inches

Worlds' End collection interior illustration

1993

Photography, Mac

3000 x 1500 pixels

Dust Covers poster.

1997

Acrylic, photography, resin, copper dust, soil, wooden frame, collage

22 x 36 inches

[L O C A T I O N] Swansea, Wales

DAVE McKEAN

Personal photographs from touring exhibition

1997

Photography

35mm

I've lived and worked in Kent for six years now.

It is silent and black at night. Recently Hale-Bopp appeared right outside my window.

You have to walk over a rickety wooden bridge to the studio. There are fish in the pond. I read in a book that if you feed your fish from the same place, at the same time, every day, then slowly, over a period of years, they will learn to come to you for food. It took my lot about a week.

Personal photograph

1997

Photograph

6 x 8 cm transparency

[L O C A T I O N] Hourglass Studio 4 : 0 0 a

Personal photograph

1997

Photography

6 x 8 cm transparency

Downstairs is for painting, drawing and constructing. Upstairs is Clare's office space, and my computer area and storage. DM

1997

Hourglass II is at a different location. It is a large 17th-century
barn and is used for photography, and recently as a film studio.

Born 1963. Attended Berkshire College of Art, 1982-86.
Several comics, some with Neil, **MR. PUNCH**, **Signal To
Noise**, some not, **ARKHAM ASYLUM** with Grant
Morrison, **Voodoo Lounge** with The Rolling Stones, **Slow
Chocolate Autopsy** with Iain Sinclair, Cages on my own.
Loads of CD covers for Michael Nyman, Tori Amos, Skinny
Puppy, Toad the Wet Sprocket, Altan, Front Line Assembly,
Bill Bruford, Bill Laswell plus.
Also kids book with Neil, **The Day I Swapped My Dad for
Two Goldfish.**
Also launch images for Kodak and Sony Playstation.
Also exhibitions in US and Europe.
Also awards.
Currently at large recording music (**Mixed Metaphors** CD),
directing short films (**The Week Before, Whack!**) and
collaborating on feature films (**The Falconer**).

1997

Thanks to Bob Watt and all at Splash of Paint Design, Thiele, all at CPL, Reading and all at Pinpoint Photography, Heathfield, who have all contributed by photographing the original works patiently and faithfully. Thanks to all at Ashford Scanning and Vector Computers for computery, scannery business of the highest order (?).

Thanks to the models: Gaiman, Neil Jones, Cathy Peters, Tim Hobday and Victoria Clarke.

A huge and hairy thank-you to Karen Berger for entrusting the shopfront to me, and to Alisa Kwitney and Shelly Roeberg for gentle reminders. A completely inadequate thank-you to Clare who has been my partner in life, crime etc. for, my God, nineteen years. Around the time of SANDMAN nos. 3 or 4, she took a major step, and decided to quit her job and run Hourglass with me. She is the reason I can spend so much time actually making things, rather than drowning in paperwork, which is what I used to do. She is also the inspiration for many of the things that get made.

Also thanks, although they'd rather have an icecream, to our joint creations Yolanda and Liam.

And finally thank you to Sandgeezer daddy and writer of evocative w'as'names, Neil — Give me a minute to catch my breath and I'm ready for the next seventy-five-issue miniseries — hello? Neil?...hello?

Sandman trading card

1993, 1997

Acrylic on photographs, Mac

2200 x 3000 pixels

Actually since I mention "paperwork," and since this is my book and I'm doing the typesetting, so I can make use of this space, a brief word to students. I now get many faxes, letters and packages from students wanting various things. It's got to the point where I just don't get around to answering them all. The best thing to do is send a questionnaire with space to answer and a stamped, addressed envelope. Anybody wanting 5000-word essays, work experience, copies of everything I've ever done or fully illustrated responses to theses, generally spend a while in my "in" tray and then either get a "sorry" postcard or get lost in the jumble. Thanks.

Sandman trading card

1995

Acrylic, copper texture, photography, Mac

800 x 1500 pixels

AND   ALL   THE   NIGHTS   ASLEE

AND   ALL   THE   COUNTED   SHEE

AND   ALL   THE   LITTLE   DEATH

AND   ALL   THE   FINAL   BREATH

THE   RUBBISH   I   HAVE   READ

DETRITUS   IN   MY   HEAD

AND   JUST   AS   I   AM   SURE

I'M   NOT   DREAMING   AFTER   ALL

I   STAY   AND   DREAM   SOME   MORE